D0286514

AGENDA FOR THEOLOGY AFTER MODERNITY ...What?

THOMAS C. ODEN

Foreword by J.I. PACKER

AGENDA FOR THEOLOGY AFTER MODERNITY ...What?

AFTER MODERNITY ... WHAT?
AGENDA FOR THEOLOGY
Copyright © 1990 by Thomas C. Oden

First softcover edition 1992

Requests for information should be addressed to:
Zondervan Publishing House
Academic and Professional Books
Grand Rapids, Michigan 49530

Library of Congress Cataloging in Publication Data

Oden, Thomas C.
    After Modernity ... what? : agenda for theology / Thomas C.
Oden
      p.   cm.
    ISBN 0-310-75391-0
    1. Theology—20th century. 2. Postmodernism—Religious
aspects—
    Christianity. 3. Liberalism (Religion)—Protestantism—
    Controversial literature.   I. Title.
    BT28.032 1990
    230–dc20   89-37637
                                                CIP

Edited by Tom Raabe and Leonard G. Goss
Designed by Leonard G. Goss and Nancy Wilson

Printed in the United States of America

92 93 94 95 96 / AM / 10 9 8 7 6 5 4 3 2

Contents

PART TWO:
THE CRITIQUE OF CRITICISM

PART THREE:
THE LIBERATION OF ORTHODOXY

Foreword by J. I. Packer

Once upon a time a band of brothers lived together beside the ocean. One day they noticed that the constant pounding of the waves was eroding the shoreline and threatening the foundations of their home. This traumatic discovery split the family. Some of the brothers felt that the only thing to do was to take ship and sail the ocean, looking for another place to live; and off they went, sadly sure that the Stay-at-Homes (as they called the siblings who would not go with them) had made a disastrous decision and would soon be homeless. The Stay-at-Homes, however, took action; they built defenses to keep the sea out, and strengthened the foundations and walls of their house, and survived, if not comfortably, at least successfully. Often they commented on how needless and misguided it had been for the Wanderers (as they called the departed ones) to take off and go to sea as they did.

For many years the Wanderers and the Stay-at-Homes were out of touch, and neither group knew for sure what had happened to the other. So it was a great day when some Stay-at-Homes patrolling the beach saw a weatherbeaten craft heading for the shore and recognized its occupant. Yes! one of the far-travelled Wanderers had come home. The reunion, though joyous on both sides, was a bit awkward at first, for the Wanderer behaved as travellers often do: he told traveller's tales, talked of many things that his brothers had not thought of before, and maintained a cheerful liveliness that was quite a contrast to the Stay-at-Home's air of defensive stolidity. But in the end they got on well, for the Stay-at-Homes came to appreciate their gadfly brother who so effectively kept them awake, and there was never any doubt that the Wanderer had come home to stay, and to help keep the old house standing firm.

I am tempted to end my foreword here, but parables are sometimes misunderstood, so I will say something more.

> We shall not cease from exploration
> And the end of all our exploring
> Will be to arrive where we started
> And know the place for the first time.

This oracle, spoken by T. S. Eliot of spiritual pilgrimage in general, finds striking illustration in the current flow of ex-liberals—tamed Wanderers, we may call them, as Reinhold Niebuhr once called himself a tamed cynic—who are returning to the practice of Christian theology in the classical Bible-based, Christ-centered, church-related, world-changing manner. Professor Oden calls it the *conciliar* method; the Reformed tend to label it the *churchly* method; and I claim it as the authentic *evangelical* method. What it does is set up a three-way conversation in which the Christian heritage of understanding—tradition, that is—is given its proper place alongside the world in hermeneutical dialogue with the infallible Scriptures. This is not Romanism, in which tradition is treated at key points as an infallible interpreter of the Bible, nor is it Fundamentalism, in which the essentially secular mind-set of post-Enlightenment rationalism is all too successfully aped, with unhappy results for the Scriptures; it is simply the historic Christian way of doing theology.

As today more and more of the Stay-at-Homes are strengthening their grip on this method, so more and more of the Wanderers, seasick more or less from long years of riding the swells and lurching into the whirlpools of modernity, are returning to it. In this book Thomas Oden reveals himself as one such.

Welcome home, brother!

Preface to This Edition:
Agenda for Theology in Ten-Year Retrospect

After Modernity . . . What? Agenda for Theology (1989) is a revision of *Agenda for Theology: Recovering Christian Roots (1979)*. The *Agenda* of 1979 used the term *postmodern* as a central organizing category before the deconstructionists had virtually nullified that term for good and all, and before they gained widespread influence in American religious circles.

In the years since 1979 the term *postmodern* has been pounced upon and taken captive by the followers of certain Continental writers (Lyotard, Theofilakis, Foucault, Derrida, contra Habermas), who just about ruined the term for any other useful purpose. It is only fair for the reader to realize, however, that I was corrupting that term before these writers published their major controversial works to corrupt it more widely.

Before I made "postmodern" central to my argument in 1979 the basic idea had been employed in a different way (yet without explicitly using the term *postmodern*) by the tradition following Friedrich Gogarten, Dietrich Bonhoeffer, and Carl Michalson. Thus it has now become necessary for me to show how what I called postmodern in the 1970s differs from what is commonly called postmodern in the 1980s.

The present edition shifts the argument toward the critique of criticism and postcritical interpretation. The language has shifted from postmodern to postcritical, since the term *postmodern* has come to have the meaning of "ultramodern" among so many deconstructionists.

I remain deeply grateful for the undeserved interest that people continue to express in *Agenda for Theology* and am appreciative of the amazing desire for its continued availability. I am now pleased to see it appear in substantially revised form. I only hope that this edition is not perceived as a lesser version of the earlier one, for I think the substantive agenda has been strengthened.

11

When asked to republish it ten years after original publication, I knew that the earlier argument could not simply be restated without major amendments. The further I got into it, the clearer it became that it required a thoroughgoing picayunish paragraph-by-paragraph revision, but not a dramatic thematic or fundamental conceptual or theoretical revision.

Hardly a single page of the former *Agenda* remains untouched in this revision. Many sections are substantially reworked. Four entirely new chapters (5–8, excluding the "Interlude") are added. The order of the material is somewhat shifted around. Yet this is not a total reconceptualization as if starting anew, but a serious revision which seeks to make the argument more pertinent for the situation now prevailing, omitting some materials and allusions less pertinent than they were a decade ago.

While not abandoning my former audience, I am now seeking more deliberately to address a wider audience of evangelicals and neo-evangelicals who may have missed the first edition. American Protestant publishing has been sharply divided into an odd-looking bird with left and right wings perched with two clutches of eggs atop the two houses of Protestantism. This work seeks now to find the audience dwelling in the other house.

The language and allusions are shifted somewhat in the direction of lay readers instead of primarily clergy. And it is shifted toward those who have an ongoing fascination with the comic premises at work in contemporary guild theology.

More surprising to me as I have made this revision is how little of the deeper substance really needs to be changed and how confident I remain with those basic intuitions that emerged in my mind with force in the mid-1970s and built to the crescendo that had become a cymbal clash by 1979.

Biblical quotations, unless otherwise noted, are from *The New English Bible*, used by permission of the Delegates of the Oxford University Press and the Syndics of the Cambridge University Press, 1961, 1970.

Introduction:
What Is Theology Coming To?

A plastic plumbing fixtures tycoon inherited from his Slavic uncle a baroque antique jeweled diadem of spectacular beauty and antiquity. He had been entrusted to take care of it but knew nothing of its actual value. He did not lift a finger to protect it. He considered it "junk." He hung it on an antelope horn on his mantel. Once in a while he enjoyed spinning it in the air, showing it off at employee parties, bending it out of shape, getting laughs. On certain occasions when in debt, he had been known to dig a jewel out and pawn it.

Isn't this much like the relationship modern persons have with classical Christianity? As heirs of modernity, we feel enormously superior to our Christian heritage. It is of little practical value to us, though we are still willing to keep it around. We would hardly feel good about throwing it away altogether, but it is little more to us than a mantel decoration or a souvenir of a trip taken long ago to Atlantic City.

The plastics magnate had received this diadem without any struggle or cost on his part, yet it had great cultural and political significance to his immigrant uncle's family and nation. The magnate was hardly aware that there had been a time when legions were willing to fight and die just to touch or behold this very diadem. This rule pertains: What we have received without cost is easily undervalued. What we ourselves have had to struggle to win or protect, we value more.

Similarly, with Christianity if we are to understand its original meaning or value, we must come once again to see it through the eyes of those who have had to struggle for it and maintain it. It is from the martyrs, saints, and prophets of Christian history, more than from recent riskless interpreters, that we learn of the value of classical Christianity. Without

13

their instruction, Christianity becomes a mere recollection, a bored nodding of the head, the source of an occasional laugh, or, in emergency, an item to pawn.

The tycoon had a son who had always been curiously attracted to the diadem, wondered about it, and for some reason thought it was incomparably beautiful. When the son came of age, he made it his purpose to learn everything he could about the crown. To his amazement, he found that for centuries it had been passed down from generation to generation as a revered symbol of the corporate identity, dignity, and freedom of a small, struggling group of patriots who had fought against great odds for their right to tend mountain vineyards in a small, faraway land.

Just such a discovery is taking place in Christian awareness today. The sons and daughters of modernity are rediscovering the neglected beauty of classical Christian teaching. It is a moment of joy, of beholding anew what had been nearly forgotten, of hugging a lost child.

This is the untold story of recent Christian thought. It is hard to see because it is a search for roots, and roots are by definition underneath the surface. Popular media perceptions of religious events see only the surface, where apparently little is happening today in religious communities. But much is happening deep below the quiet façade.

I have been astonished to discover that some of my best students, those who have most profoundly grasped the hopes of modernity, fought for its political dreams, understood its psychological interpretations, lived out its symbols, experienced its technological achievements and failures, its hedonic ecstasies and spiritual hungers—these keenest, most perceptive students are the ones most insistent on letting the ancient tradition speak for itself. They have had a bellyful of the hyped claims of modern therapies and political messianism to make all things right. They are fascinated—and often passionately moved—by the primitive language of the apostolic tradition and the ancient Christian writers, undiluted by our contemporary efforts to soften it or make it easier or package it for smaller challenge but greater acceptability.

Finally my students got through to me. They do not want to hear a watered-down modern reinterpretation. They want nothing less than the substance of the faith of the apostles and martyrs without too much interference from modern pablum-peddlers who doubt that they are tough enough to take it straight. They do not mind occasionally hearing my opinions, but they would rather spend their valuable time listening directly to Paul's letter to Rome, to Irenaeus on heresy, to Cyprian on martyrdom, to the great ecumenical councils defining the heart of belief, to Anselm struggling to reason about God's existence, to Luther addressing the German nobility, or to Wesley writing his journal between long days on horseback.

This is what our students do not want to miss: a chance to experience the power of straightforward Christian testimony in the presence of a community of living faith, without heavy distortions by modern assumptions about what Christianity has recently been imagined to be. When we give them anything less, they experience a sense of dilution, a feeling that they have been cheated, that something crucial has been left out of their education.

This cannot be explained simply as an afterburn of authoritarianism or a new flaring up of the charismatic impulse, or a hunger for a past pietism, or a nostalgia for a more stable society (although any of these influences may at times be felt). Rather, to our surprise, we are now meeting in our worshiping communities the postcritical student who has already imbibed deeply of the best wellsprings of the finest modern universities and come away thirsty, who has gone through the long smorgasbord of pop psychologies and political ideologies and various alterations of consciousness by music, chemistry, and social experiment, and who now hungers for more nourishing food. This student may know well the rigor of the scientific laboratory but is quite clear that its results will not resurrect faith or save the soul. We are dealing with a student who has been through the best the university has to offer and now is searching for a way to reconstruction, a way of return, a way of purgation.

These students have explored the edges and precipices of the ecstasies of modern freedom and have fallen into their share of its abysses. Having painfully experienced the limits of modernity, they are now engaging in a lengthy pilgrimage in which they have at long last stumbled, almost by accident, on the texts and spiritual directions and confessions and

liturgies of classical Christianity. They have grown up in a
moral milieu in which that ancient Christian tradition has
been either ridiculed or sentimentalized or sugarcoated or
made the butt of a joke. But they know its deeper joy has
hardly been touched.

This is what I mean by the postcritical orthodoxy. Its spirit
is embodied in the student who has been through the
challenges of university education, sometimes through the
hazards of the drug scene, through the ups and downs of
sweaty political or ideological engagement, through the head
shrinks and group thinks of popular therapies, and through a
dozen sexual messianisms, only to become weary of the
pretentious motions of frenetic change. At length these
travelers have come upon Christ's living presence in the
world in an actual community of Christians and now have set
out to understand what has happened to them in light of the
classical texts of Scripture and tradition.

Not all the postcritical inquirers are students. Some are
driving cabs or growing cabbage or playing gigs or repairing
Hondas or testing radon or practicing law. It just happens that
my personal vantage point for meeting them has been in a
theological seminary, where they come to me on the rebound
from profound disillusionments with modern trends and a
hunger for spiritual roots.

The current generation of postcritical students asks far
deeper questions than their religious mentors are prepared to
answer on the basis of the prevailing theologies of recent
Protestantism. They spot empty rhetoric a mile away. They
will not abide easy evasions or cheap reassurances. They
want substance, not pablum. They may have their blind spots,
but their hearing is perfect in the presence of double-talk. I
know how penetrating their criticisms can be. I teach them
daily. They expect us to deliver to them the available power
of the Christian heritage rather than trendy ideas of minor
modern heretics.

These young people, whose hopes and intuitions will be
explored in these pages, remain the unreported story of this
period of American religious life. The popular press can see
no reportable news here. But if one of these young people
were to swallow a fish or crack someone on the head with a
sign with a four-letter word on it or announce with gestures of

importance that he or she had discovered a new coital position, you can bet that would be vigorously reported. But that is the nature of "news," and it is the very reason why religious teaching does well to pay less and less attention to the press's view of theological importance. When the media become fixated only on aberrations, especially among those who imagine that they constitute some irrepressible wave of the future, they unconsciously collude with the encouragement of publicity for anyone who is odd, provocative, scandalous, or has his or her hat on backward. This discussion is in part simply a report of what I am finding in the moral and intellectual appetites of the emerging generation of young people, especially of those preparing for Christian ministry. I am hoping to sharpen these conceptions and rectify misconceptions.

PART ONE:

THE COURTSHIP OF
MODERNITY

What is happening in theology today? Imagine a person who has been chronically sick, jaundiced, and immobilized by an unidentified virus. A powerful antibiotic has recently been injected into the bloodstream. On the surface it appears as though the patient is sick unto death, with no treatment known. But the potent healing force is already speeding to relieve, covertly at work, beginning to battle the infection day and night. The patient, however, remains miserable, and there is no obvious indication yet that a turning point has been reached.

1

In and Out of Season

So What Else Is New?

What follows is for some readers best to be viewed under the genre of entertainment. It should be tasted, not masticated—taken more like broth than beef—and if anyone should decide to proceed further it would be best to do so in the spirit of proximate, not ultimate, seriousness. For the last thing the faith needs is another absolutely serious new program of theology. Theological programs have come and gone at an embarrassing rate in the last two decades. I would prefer to disclaim any expectations that such might be my purpose. The only program that conceivably might serve some useful purpose would be a counterprogrammatic theology, if that could be imagined—a program whose sole purpose is to end theology programs.

So, if it already looks as if I am proposing a new reform of theology, that would be a mistaken guess. Theology needs reforming but not in a new way, only in an old and familiar way. The reform-minded are not likely to gain much comfort from the curious notions that Christian teaching needs to be reformed in the direction of antiquity, or that modernity is already way out of date, or that the cheap promise of radical newness is the most boring and repetitious of all modern ideas. These curious notions are my fascination and the preoccupation of my students.

21

The Dream of Unoriginality

I once had a curious dream. The scene was in the New
Haven cemetery, where I accidentally stumbled over my own
tombstone, only to be confronted by this bemusing epitaph:
"He made no new contribution to theology."

I woke up feeling deeply reassured, for I have been trying
in my own way to follow the strict mandate of Irenaeus "not
to invent new doctrine." No concept was more deplored by
the early ecumenical councils than the notion that theology's
task was to "innovate" (*neoterizein*). That implied some
imagined creative addition to the apostolic teaching and thus
something "other than" (*heteros*) the received doctrine
(*doxa*), "the baptism into which we have been baptized."

What the ancient church teachers *least* wished for a
theology was that it would be "fresh" or "self-expressive" or
an embellishment of purely private inspirations, as if these
might stand as some "decisive improvement" on the apostolic
teaching.

Yet from the first day I ever thought of becoming a
theologian I have been earnestly taught and admonished that
my most urgent task was to "think creatively" so as to make
"some new contribution" to theology. Nothing at Yale was
drummed into my head more firmly than that the theology I
would seek would be my own, and my uniqueness would
imprint it. So you can imagine that it took no small effort on
my part to resist the repeated reinforcements of my best
education in order to overcome the constant temptation to
novelty. And you can understand how relieved I was to see
such an intriguing epitaph prefigured in a dream, one that at
last seems to be coming true on these pages—"to make no
new contribution to theology"—*Laus Deo*.

The Revisionists

Fantasize, if you will, a large group of energetic scholars
who call themselves "Islamic theologians," but who never
pray, seldom bother to read the Koran, and in their private
moments derisively mock Muhammad with clever panto-
mimes that suggest that he was little more than a silly,

neurotic egotist; yet who nonetheless insist vehemently that they represent the true tradition of Islamic spirituality.

Suppose that the secret passion of these scholars is actually the study of Freud. They have taken carefully selected passages of the Koran and medieval Islamic texts and radically reinterpreted them in a Freudian fashion, showing their oedipal ambivalences, repressed sexuality, totemic symbolism, the cathexis of wish formations, subtle forms of sublimation, and so on, so that the final result was a blatant Freudianization of Islam. Of course, all the moral imperatives would then have to go, the sociological substance of the Islamic tradition would obviously be found dispensable, all ideas of revelation would have to be dismissed. Yet suppose these scholars held fast to the pretense that they were the true arbiters of Islamic teaching. Don't laugh too quickly; such a reversal is entirely possible. In fact, I would not be surprised if a group of scholars in some university in Algiers or Islamabad were currently working along just such "constructive" lines.

Suppose you were advising a serious Christian theological student who had become fascinated with Islam, and who wanted to go abroad to learn all he could about the true spirit of Islam—would you even for a moment consider sending him to these seeming "Islamic theologians"? More likely you would advise him to go instead to one of the renowned historical centers of traditional Islamic prayer, legal study, archival deposits, and Islamic theology. Most of all you would hope that he would somehow find his way into a vibrant, pulsating community of genuine Islamic faith so as to get directly in touch with the creative energies of Islam that have flowed through the centuries. And if he had heard somewhere of the Freudian Muslims and was curiously fascinated by them, you would wisely advise him that if he were interested merely in pseudo-Islamic curiosities, they might be given some attention, but if he were interested in the vital tradition of Islam devoutly believed by millions, he would do well to understand it historically as a living community of prayer, instead of a twisted plaything seen through the heavily coated lens of modernity.

Yet something like Freudianized Islam has proliferated and taken deep root in modern Christianity. We have seen the language of Christianity tamed by the civil religionists, neatly pruned by the logical positivists, "dehistoricized" by the existentialists, "deabsolutized" by the process theologians, naturalized by behaviorists, sentimentalized by the situation ethicists, made into chemistry by the drug-oriented spiritualists, secularized by the "death of God" partisans, politicized by social activists, and set free from all bonds by the sexual liberationists. In each case, they rebaptized Christianity in the triune name of the nineteenth, twentieth, and twenty-first centuries. (One can almost visualize each movement being solemnly immersed three times under water with the sacred numbers of the three centuries being gravely intoned by a psychiatrist, guru, or spiritual adept on a sandy beach in a late summer evening with mantric intonations echoing over the waves.)

But Christianity is not now and has not since the seventeenth century been fairly judged exclusively by its *au courant* manifestations. Rather, it is to be properly judged and understood by its primitive formation, and especially by those periods of its historical development that have given the most careful attention to the original vitalities of its primitive formation. Hence Christianity is not to be judged by what a majority (even a large majority) of contemporary theologians might say is true Christianity if they forgetfully depart from Scripture and ancient ecumenical tradition.

A Reversal of Consciousness

An unexpected learning occurred the day I had to pack up my books for shipment to the distant spot where I was to spend a change-of-pace research year. I was to be away from my personal library for an entire year, a prospect that gives any bibliophile teeth-rattling separation anxieties. I was forced to make harsh choices about which volumes I would take and which I would leave behind. If I shipped too many books, the cost would be atrocious.

As I began to make my second-and-third-round eliminations, an astonishing pattern became apparent to me. Among the books reserved for shipment I was picking Aeschylus, Clement of Alexandria, Epictetus, Tertullian, Nemesius, John

Chrysostom, Augustine, Boethius, Dante, Hugh of St. Victor, Anselm, and so on. Many of these books I had already read, but they seemed important to take with me.

Finally the shock hit me: there were no books among my final selections from the twentieth century! The most recent ones in my shipment list were J. H. Newman, Phoebe Palmer, and William Burt Pope. Did that mean that I was bored with twentieth-century literature? Hardly, for I teach several courses and enjoy teaching them in twentieth-century thought. The truth is, however, that I found the premodern writers more personally significant for my growth, more crucial for my personal being, than the full range of scientific and literary achievements of the twentieth century.

I learned something important about myself on that fateful day. It felt as though the second Christian millennium was already over for me spiritually. It was as if it had burned itself out several years before its expected demise.

If I had to assign a date to my entrance into the "postmodern" world (similar to the way the frontier revivalists used to speak of the exact day they were converted), I think it would be that day when I had to choose the books I most needed, and most certainly wanted with me, and discovered to my astonishment that if push came to shove I could do without the twentieth-century material altogether, but that I could not seem to do without Hippolytus, Thomas Aquinas, Nicholas of Cusa, *Theologia Germanica*, Maimonides, Pascal, and Kierkegaard.

The Flight from Boredom

The present mood of academic theology is boredom. One cannot help but wonder, purely out of humane interest, whether there might be some therapy for this boredom. There seems to be no lack of a certain kind of brilliance among those who view themselves as theologians, and plodding persistence among many others, but the mind often seems to have lost heart and the body to have lost soul.

Admittedly, theology has managed to gain a modest status in the harsh world—a chair here or there in a sprawling tax-supported university or the sporadic attention of the media (focused selectively on demonstration politics, homosexuality, drugs, and death). For half a century, theologians have been earnestly longing and wishing and even praying (well, that might be an exaggeration) for a little more respectability in the eyes of modernity. They have not asked for the moon. Even one tiny step up the academic pecking order would have been savored immensely.

So teachers of religion have developed huge upwardly mobile professional societies that are carbon copies of other professional societies. The field has even managed to obtain a convenient name change—from theology to religious studies. More government grants, they said. It has seemed "a decisive step ahead" to say that theology's subject matter is no longer, strictly speaking, God or Holy Writ or revelation but religious experience viewed comparatively. Even though religion departments remain near-pariahs in most universities, it can be fairly reported that the field of religious studies now holds a tiny beachhead in the modern secular university.

This is no small achievement, but has it led to a sense of fulfillment, integrity, or satisfaction in this academic bailiwick? Apparently not, judged by the depression-proneness and vocational egress rate in this professional arena. Even amid its apparent secular successes, the question lingers: How is theology to find true happiness in the modern world? Such a theme might even be worthy of an afternoon soap opera. What is theology now to do with its newfound freedom from Holy Writ and revelation and church and antiquity?

The "Movement" Theologian

In order to sharpen my portrayal of theology's amiable accommodation to modernity, I will describe a particular individual, an ordained theologian whom I have known for a long time and whose career until recently can only be described as that of a "movement person." If I appear to go into needless detail about this person, it is nonetheless useful to learn of the specifics of what I mean by an addictive accommodationism. In his pursuit of movements, his overall pattern was diligently to learn from them, to throw himself into them, and then eventually to baptize them insofar as they showed any remote kinship with Christianity, and then to turn to another movement.

Now well into middle age, our subject took his first plunge into "movement identity" at sixteen when he joined the United World Federalists to promote world government through various educational and church groups. From 1954 (when he attended the Evanston Assembly) to 1966 (at the Geneva World Conference on Church and Society) he was much involved in ecumenical debate, promotion, and organization. His deepening involvement in the civil rights movement began at about seventeen and four years later was intensified by his attendance at the national NAACP convention in 1953 and by subsequent participation in marches, demonstrations, pray-ins, sit-ins, letter campaigns, and other forms of political activism.

More than a decade before the Vietnam War, our "movement theologian" was an active pacifist, struggling to motivate the antiwar movement during the difficult McCarthy days. The fact that he understood himself as a democratic socialist and theoretical Marxist during the McCarthy period did not make his task any easier. He spearheaded the first Students for Democratic Action group to be organized in his conservative home state in the early 1950s. By the mid-1950s he was active in the American Civil Liberties Union; in the pre-NOW women's rights movement as an advocate of liberalized abortion; and as a steady opponent of states' rights, military spending, and bourgeois morality. His movement identity took a new turn in the late 1950s when he became enamored with the existentialist movement, immersing himself particularly in the demythologization movement, writing his doctoral dissertation on its chief theorist.

The early 1960s found him intimately engaged in the client-centered therapy movement. Later he became engrossed in Transactional Analysis and soon was actively participating in the Gestalt therapy movement, especially through Esalen connections. His involvement deepened in the "third force" movement in humanistic psychology, struggling to move beyond psychoanalysis and behaviorism, as he contributed to its journals and experimented with its therapeutic strategies in his theological school classrooms. This was supplemented by several years of involvement in the T-

Group movement associated with the National Training Laboratories, which he tried to integrate into his religious views. In the early 1970s, he joined a society for the study of paranormal phenomena, taught a class in parapsychology, and directed controlled research experiments with mung beans, Kirlian photography, biorhythm charts, pyramids, tarot cards, and the correlation of astrological predictions with the daily ups and downs of behavior.

My purpose in reciting this long litany is not to boast, for indeed I am that wandering theologian, less proud than amused by the territory I have covered. Rather, the purpose is to recite a straightforward description of what at least one mainline Protestant theologian conceived to be his task in successive phases of the last few decades.

So when I am speaking of a diarrhea of religious accommodation, I am not thinking of "the other guys" or speaking in the abstract, but out of my own personal history. I do not wish contritely to apologize for my twenty-five years as a movement person, because I learned so much and encountered so many bright and beautiful persons. But I now experience the afterburn of "movement" existence, of messianic pretensions, of self-congratulatory idealisms. It is understandable, after this roller-coaster ride, that I would be drawn to a "postmovement" sociology of continuity, maintenance, and legitimation, hoping to ameliorate the "movement psychology" of immediate change. The very thinkers I once excoriated as "conservative" (the Burkes, the Newmans, the Thomists) I now find annually increasing in plausibility, depth, and wisdom.

The shocker is not merely that I rode so many bandwagons, but that I thought I was doing Christian teaching a marvelous favor by it and at times considered this accommodation the very substance of the Christian teaching office. While Christian teaching must not rule out any investigations of truth or active involvement to embody it, it should be wary lest it reduce Christian doctrine to these movements, and it should be better prepared to discern which movements are more or less an expression of Christ's ministry to the world.

It was the abortion-on-demand movement more than anything else that brought me to movement revulsiveness. The climbing abortion statistics made me movement-weary, movement-demoralized. I now suspect that a fair amount of my own idealistic history of political action was ill conceived by self-deceptive romanticisms, in search of power in the form of prestige, that were from the beginning willing to destroy human traditions in the name of humanity and at the end willing to extinguish the futures of countless unborn children in the name of individual autonomy. So, reflected in the mirror of my own history, I see my own generation and my children's generation of movement idealisms as naively proud and sadly misdirected, despite good intentions. If I have grown wary about movement people, it is because I am wary of the consequences of my own good intentions.

Meanwhile, in the period before the reversal, my intellectual dialogue remained embarrassingly constricted almost exclusively to university colleagues and liberal churchmen, the only club I knew. When I later discovered among brilliant Protestant evangelicals a superb quality of exegesis, I wondered why it took so long. And when I found in Roman Catholic friends a marvelous depth of historical and moral awareness, I wondered what it was in my academic and church tradition that prevented my meeting them, or that systematically cut me off from dialogue with them, and why my latitudinarian tradition had been so defensive toward them. All these questions are subjects for further historical and sociological investigation, but they arise out of a vague sense of grief over lost possibilities and out of confusion that a church tradition that spoke so often about tolerance and universality could be so intolerant and parochial.

2

Full Circle

The philosophical center of modernity is no dark secret. It
is a narcissistic hedonism that assumes that moral value is
reducible to now feelings and sensory experience. It views
human existence essentially as spiritless body, sex as orgasm,
psychology as amoral data gathering, and politics as the
manipulation of power. It systematically ignores the human
capacity of self-transcendence, moral reasoning, covenant
commitment, and self-sacrificial *agape*.

These axiomatic assumptions prevail among the intellectual elite that has of late become the apple of many a parson's
eye. While the mainline religious leadership should have
been giving them what it distinctively has to give—namely,
firm, critical resistance rooted in a historical perspective that
modernity could find instructive—instead the religious leadership withheld its gift and whored after each successive
stage of modernity's profligacy. While its lusty affair with
modernity has been going on for about two centuries, it has
not been until the last quarter century that there has been a
wholesale devaluation of the currency of Christian language,
symbolism, teaching, and witness—a total sellout and bankruptcy to support the fixed habits of modern addictions.

Young people are beginning to be vaguely aware of the
depth of the sellout, the urgency to redirect the momentum,
and the fatefulness of their calling at this nexus of history.

31

The collusions are intricate. A fair amount of courage is required even to face the problem.

Modernity: How Long Will We Tolerate Its Illusions?

The faddism of theology in the past three decades was not accidental—it was necessary *if* you understand theology to be a constant catch-up process, trying to keep pace with each new ripple of the ideological river. What else could theology become but faddist, under such a definition?

The same addiction that has degenerated modern art has also infected theology. The marvelous tradition of Cezanne, Braque, Picasso, and Chagall has withered into a speedway race of faddists who have placed such a high value on "doing something different" (no matter what) that artistic excellence has been lost in the frantic search for novelty. An inversion of value has occurred in which the highest value is placed not on aesthetic imagination, craft, meaning, or beauty but on novelty—*"Dadaism"*—and compulsive uniqueness. The more outrageous it is, the more "creative" it is viewed by connoisseurs, and the more boring it is to most of us. When novelty becomes the chief criterion of artistic quality, we can only chuckle at the expensive wool being pulled over someone's eyes.

Exactly the same has happened in religious studies with its new theologies every spring season, a wide assortment of "new moralities," "new hermeneutics," and (note how the adjectives suddenly have to be pumped up) "revolutionary breakthroughs." On closer inspection, however, the reader discovers that all these views may be found in the books of decades ago, except then with mercifully fewer pretensions and less hysteria.

We have blithely proceeded on the skewed assumption that in theology—just as in corn poppers, electric toothbrushes, and automobile exhaust systems—new is good, newer is better, and newest is best. The correction of this distorted analogy will have a shocking effect on seminary campuses long habituated to instant theology. The irony is that these "most innovative" seminaries are regarded in certain circles as better just to that degree that they follow this debilitating assumption. So the "best" ones have by this logic cut themselves systematically off from sustained discourse with classical Christianity. But if Protestantism should learn again to work at the distinction between heterodoxy and orthodoxy, what effect would it have on pastoral care, Christian education, preaching, biblical studies, administrative oversight, social ethics, and so on? The possibilities are staggering.

The fundamental eros of the leading contemporary theological traditions of Bultmann, Tillich, Bonhoeffer, Whitehead, and Rahner is accommodation to modernity. This is the underlying motif that unites the seemingly vast differences between many forms of existential theology, process theology, liberation theology, and demythologization—all are searching for some more compatible adjustment to modernity.

The spirit of accommodation has not prevailed without occasional minority voices and skirmishes, but the resistance to it has been divided and defensive: Some Roman Catholic holdouts and a few Anglo-Catholics and evangelicals have offered sporadic resistance to the wholesale accommodation of Christianity to modernity, but they often seem like living anachronisms. Political and philosophical conservatism has offered some resistance, but it has sometimes been coupled with political programs that seem to deny much of classical Christianity's concern for the poor.

The flurry of Barthian-Niebuhrian neoorthodoxy, whose season lengthened only to a few fleeting decades, never gained much grass-roots ecclesial strength and had its chief influence in a few key seminaries where it has by now mostly dissipated. Fundamentalism has been more effective in nurturing intergenerational communities of faith, but its influence has been unevenly local and regional, and it has hardly affected the vast cities of modernity. Pacifist sects such as the Amish have literally withdrawn from modernity and will have nothing to do with it. No cars, no condoms, no buttons, no mass media, and so on. Even if we should admire their spirit and tenacity, we are far too habituated to the technologies and assumptions of modernity to join them on their rigorous and lonely path.

A more influential model for postcritical orthodox Christians: postcritical orthodox Jews. Often the sons and daughters of immigrants who gave enormous energies to finding their way into American upward mobility, the present generation has tripped radically into the far edges of modern experimental consciousness, only eventually to find their way back into the marvelous Jewish heritage that their grandfathers had to suppress temporarily and at times disavow. Like young Jews reidentifying with orthodoxy, young Christians are now trying to become astute gardeners of their tradition, learning to transplant the ancient faith in the fresh soil of modernity.

Meanwhile, they are learning that some seeds spuriously marketed as "Christian" in the modern ideological supermarket produce a fruit quite different from life in Christ. These youthful inquirers are now trying to nurture along seeds from a few remaining plants that have endured through the ravages of modernity. They are carefully tending, cultivating, and protecting the rare plants that come from genuine seeds that differ so completely from those of tasteless, fabricated modern claimants.

The agenda for theology at the end of the twentieth century, following the steady deterioration of a hundred years and the disaster of the last few decades, is to begin to prepare the postmodern Christian community for its third millennium by returning again to the careful study and respectful following of the central tradition of classical Christian exegesis.

It will require energetic historical inquiry into the internal reasonings of classical Christian orthodoxy, a new gift of empathy for alternative forms of historical consciousness, and an ability to discern what is and what is not within the core. Ministry will have to learn anew a skill that once was taken for granted but now has become long forgotten—the ability to distinguish between doctrinal truth and error. It is a discernment too long neglected. It raises questions that we have too long pretended did not exist. If we do not learn this discernment, our grandchildren will find it ever more difficult. It may take the grandchild generation of Christians half a century to rebuild from the ruins of the cultural devastations we leave.

The Ruins of Modern Chauvinism

Instead of modernity discrediting Christian faith as advertised, modernity itself is unexpectedly in the process of being discredited. The shallows of modernity only make it more urgent to explore the depths of Christian hope and love. We have overassessed modernity's power to deliver and underassessed its inner contradictions and limits.

Out of that vast miscalculation, the advocates of modernity in every generation since Voltaire have repeatedly announced the imminent demise of religion. One would think that this tiresome prognostication would at some time finally be considered refuted or at least ignored. But the expectation of the end of religion seems indefatigable, despite all evidences to the contrary.

It was not until the last quarter century that professors and ministers of religion in fairly large numbers began to cast their lot with the prognosis of Voltaire. Yet, far from disposing of Christian orthodoxy, modernity has now come full circle. Against all its self-expectations it is now having to face up to its own interpersonal bankruptcy, social neuroses, and moral vacuity.

The religious challenge to young people today as they approach Christianity's third millennium is to end the defensive mentality of retreat and failure of nerve. They are gaining fresh courage. It is first of all a courage to say no. They realize that they stand in the presence of a rapidly deteriorating modern ethos that has lost its moral power. Increasing numbers of young people are no longer willing to buy into the assumption that modernity holds a legitimate moral authority over Christian conscience, Christian language, and Christian child-care.

If we should ever imagine that modernity's suffering might be lessened by the retreat of Christianity from its central convictions, we would have misunderstood modernity as badly as Christianity. If classical Christian faith should become temporarily lost and obliterated, it would be modernity's loss as much as Christianity's. If we should ever in moments of demoralization fantasize that the finest contribution Christianity could make to modernity would be to abandon its great tradition—against which a frustrated modernity has always had to struggle—then we should fear most not for the fate of Christianity (whose continuity is already assured by God's own promise) but for modernity without Christianity's compassionate realism. Even the secularization process has received its moral vitality from its constant companion, orthodox Christianity.

A strong awareness is dawning amid the ruins of modern sexual and familial disorder. It is time to quit our groveling apologies for traditional Christianity. It is time to listen intently to the scriptural texts and early Christian writers. It is time to ask how classical Christianity itself might teach us to understand the providence of God in the midst of our broken and confused modern situation.

This is why our students are reading classical Christian interpretations of history (from the *Church History* of Eusebius and Augustine's *City of God* through Calvin and Milton to Kierkegaard's *The Present Age*) with far greater eagerness today than anyone would have expected. They come off looking pretty good in relation to pop modern chauvinist interpreters of history such as Alvin Toffler of a few years ago.

By *modern chauvinist* I mean those whose historical perspective, loyalties, and attachments are so strictly limited to modern values that they impulsively denigrate all premodern wisdoms. Modern chauvinism assumes the intrinsic inferiority of all premodern thought and the consequent superiority of modern thought.

Christianity does not rejoice in the failure or success of modernity. But neither does Christianity need to assume that its destiny is ultimately bound up with the failure or success of modernity. It is just because we have tried to become successful on modernity's terms that we have contracted theological vertigo. It is not surprising that we should now be quietly mourning the loss of our own surest form of accountability to modernity—faithfulness to canonical Scripture and classical consensual exegesis, which have provided the deepest perennial spiritual wellsprings of modern consciousness and the best source of its survivability.

Consensual, Conciliar Orthodoxy

Classical Christianity has never said that the believer cannot inquire into scientific understandings of reality or probe the edges of undiscovered truth or refine the methods of research to the tiniest caliber. Rather, it has celebrated the hope that all the varied dimensions of truth awaiting our discovery are more profoundly understandable and make wiser sense within the frame of reference of the meaning of universal history. This meaning Christians believe to be revealed in Jesus' resurrection.

There is nothing in the orthodox Jewish or Christian tradition that prohibits the modern mind from feeding its computers with the most complex data, sorting out the conflicted energies of the human psyche, refining the methods of historical investigation, or experimenting with the expansion of consciousness through meditation. These are rather to be enjoyed and celebrated, especially when seen in relation to the end of history, which for Christians and Jews is ultimately expected as an event of resurrection beyond all human alienations.

By *classical Christianity* (or ancient ecumenical orthodoxy), I mean the Christian consensus of the first millennium. A fuller statement of that consensus awaits chapter 13, but it must be asked, in a preliminary way, What is orthodoxy? In brief, it is that faith to which Vincent of Lérins pointed in the concise phrase *quod ubique, quod semper, quod ab omnibus creditum est* ("that which has been everywhere and always and by everyone believed"). It is the faith generally shared by all Christians, especially as defined in the crucial early periods of Christian doctrinal definition.

These definitions were not written by individuals but were hammered out by synods, councils, and consensual bodies. On at least seven notable occasions, they met on a worldwide basis to express the universal consent of the believing church to the apostolic teaching as defined, and left as a legacy the seven ecumenical councils that have been accepted by the entire church as normative for almost two millennia.

The seven councils commonly bound all Christians both in East and West and were received with universal Christian consent. They are (with dates and chief subjects): (1) Nicaea (325, Arianism); (2) Constantinople I (381, Apollinarianism); (3) Ephesus (431, Nestorianism); (4) Chalcedon (451, Eutychianism); (5) Constantinople II (553, Three Chapters Controversy); (6) Constantinople III (680–81, Monothelitism);

and (7) Nicaea II (787, Iconoclasm). We might be led to assume that every ordained minister would be thoroughly schooled in the canons and decrees of these universally accepted councils (to be presupposed as one assumes that the multiplication tables are known by every mathematician), but that would be a rash assumption. A thorough reappraisal of the theological method implicit in these early doctrinal formulations is a crucial part of the awaiting agenda of contemporary theology.

The Cusp of the Second Millennium

The word *cuspis* (Latin) means a "pointed end or projection formed by converging curves." In horoscopy, the term *cusp* refers to the tail end of one period or the beginning of another, often a time thought to be characterized by uncertainty and volatility. We are now dwelling in the cusp of the second Christian millennium. It offers us the exceptional possibility of rethinking the meaning of the first two millennia and accepting the challenge to prepare for the third.

These words of John Watson from the Beecher Lectures of 1896 at Yale seem aimed directly at us today:

> For a quarter of a century at least, the intellectual resources of the church have been withdrawn from the study of dogma (with, of course, some brilliant exceptions) and devoted to criticism . . . . The ministers of today have been trained in this age and baptized into its spirit. We have shared the hopes and endeavors, we have felt the doubts and anxieties of our time, and we can now frankly tell our people its faults and fruits.
>
> Criticism has offended the church by its pretentiousness, for its preachers were apt to speak as if they had a new gospel. Of course they had nothing, and could have nothing, of the kind. They have given [us] a large amount of information and they have removed some traditions, but a message for the soul criticism can never offer . . . . Criticism has also sinned through uncharitableness; for some of the pioneers of the new school have forgotten good manners and have not carried themselves respectfully to the past. While a discoverer in physics is ever grateful for the work done by his predecessors, and corrects their mistakes with humility, recognizing that he stands on their shoulders and that his results will also one day be revised,

the biblical critic has been inclined to treat the old scholarship with unconcealed contempt, and to expose its errors with malignant satisfaction. (John Watson, "The New Dogma," *The Cure of Souls, 140–42*).

The theological situation in the last quarter of the twentieth century does not differ substantially from the last quarter of the nineteenth, except that the incipient habits Watson described in 1896 have now become institutionalized, normative, and thoroughly professionalized.

Disenchantment with the Enchantments of Modernity

By now, many of us are experiencing a gnawing disenchantment with the enchantments of modernity. But if the time has come to spoil the spoilers and to debunk the debunkers, let it proceed without malice and above all in good humor. This cheerful, guileless work has already long been initiated by the likes of Edwin Lewis, Reinhold Niebuhr, Will Herberg, Peter Berger, and others. But so far it has only scratched the surface. The critique has not achieved the levels of comedy or irony that the situation richly invites.

Wishing not to be misunderstood, I happily confess that I am a modern man still fascinated with the twentieth century and feel fortunate to be a part of it technologically, although I keep wondering to what depth my soul has been traded away. The scientific and technological achievements of modern life are so impressive, even awesome, that they remind us that all our mechanisms can be just as easily turned against justice and humanization as toward them. Christianity need not think backward technologically, but all of this spectacular progress in technology does not imply an inevitable ethical or spiritual progress. We are deluded when we extrapolate the "success" of the internal combustion engine and atomic power (as if they were unmixed blessings) so as to imagine that they represent an absolutely necessary momentum toward unending spiritual progress.

Admittedly, we would all prefer to go to a dentist with up-to-date equipment than one with antiquated medieval pliers. We would rather travel cross-country by air than horseback. But that does not imply that new ideas are by their newness better; or that our grandchildren, because they come later in time, are thereby destined to be morally more aware than we are; or that we are spiritually more advanced than our grandparents. It is that not-so-subtle skip in logic, the progressivist *non sequitur*, that has led modernity astray and in the process deceptively drawn Christianity into the grip of hopeless fantasies.

The paradigm of "social planning" (and of theology modeled after the dreams of social planners) has exercised undue influence on our church bureaucracies and institutions. This paradigm assumes that a single creative person can create on the drawing board a better idea of society or a better design for a social process than can history itself. This has an antipopulist, antidemocratic assumption that the actual meshing wills and competing interests of specific people struggling under the concrete limitations of unfolding history are less valuable than the rational planner.

Elitist social architects assume that the tough part is getting the right idea and the easy part is the implementation of it in actual social arrangements. So social planning (and theologies based upon it) quickly becomes an idea factory. It tends to dismiss the actualities of history and the real people that inhabit it (as Robert Moses, the dean of urban planners, underestimated the value of the ethnic neighborhoods he destroyed in the name of urban renewal).

The university establishment has fed on this fantasy, assuming that individuals looking at history from highly abstract and distanced angles would be able easily to achieve more precise and better forms of social reasoning than the actual historical process itself ever could. How pretentious to assume that the lone individual is wiser and better than the complex interests at play in a living family or neighborhood or subculture or religious tradition. Yet nothing is more characteristic of theology at the end of the second millennium than this elitist fantasy. Virtually a direct opposite of the paradigm of social planning is the implicit theological method of orthodoxy.

The Polemic against Repression

We have witnessed in these waning stages of the twentieth century a powerful polemic against what has been called repression of many kinds—sexual repression (Freud), class repression (Marx), and political repression (Marcuse). We now have seen enough of these polemicists to realize at least two things: (1) that what is called repression is often either the legitimate protest of conscience or a carefully balanced and hard-won equilibrium of social traditioning; and (2) that the social and psychological alternatives that are proposed in the name of counterrepression are themselves often more profoundly oppressive both to conscience and human community. This is one of the most harsh but most certain learnings of the pilgrimage of postmodern youth. Because they could not learn it from history, they were forced to learn from hard street experience that their high-sounding, low-slugging polemic is itself often unexpectedly even more repressive than the repression it assails.

Twentieth-century theology has too cheaply and prematurely sided with this oversimplified Marxian-Nietzschean-Freudian polemic against social and psychological repression. But this is merely the tip of the iceberg. The deeper lust of twentieth-century theology, following well-established trends of nineteenth-century religious accommodationism, has been directed toward finding some convenient means of getting itself legitimated in the eyes of modernity.

Newer = Better?

I suggest a simple test for showing that the innocent words *new* and *change* actually function like potent magic words in our current vocabulary, and with particularly surprising force in ordinary conversations: Accurately count the number of times *new* and *good* are used as synonyms.

Then ask yourself, were there any instances in which the word *change* was used in a pejorative sense? How often was it silently assumed that new = good, change = improvement? Was it assumed that if something new could be identified, it would by definition bring about a better situation? Or if some undeveloped process developed, it would thereby constitute a "leap ahead"? Or if something merely changed, it would imply a moral advancement or a virtue of some kind?

If your count is like mine, I think you will discover that these words function almost exactly like magic words have functioned in earlier societies. Some conversants will use the magic words incessantly, sprinkling them generously into nearly every reference. Others use the magic words somewhat as a kid uses body torque while playing pinball, as if to persuade the ball to go a certain way without lighting up the "tilt" sign.

Academics prefer more sophisticated synonyms, such as *emergent, innovative, revolutionary,* or *metamorphosis.* But the magic is still there. Eyes light up, bells ring, money changes hands. In fact, the overall effect of the magic words in some circles is very like a pinball fantasy victory.

The surest move I know toward postcritical consciousness consists in this simple maxim: Quit using *new* and *change* as magic words. Quitting cold turkey is, of course, difficult. But when it can be done, the reversal of consciousness is suddenly felt dramatically. I know of no better therapy for unconscious faddism.

By the same logic, modernity also has its bad magic words: Anything that looks "old hat" or "antiquated" or "rigid" or "traditional" will be subtly linked implicitly with evils to be avoided, vicious repressions that hold us down, powers of darkness. The adjectives abound—all with a stale smell: paleo-anything, medieval, obsolete, senile, elderly, bygone, extinct.

Check it out for yourself. Plot in two columns on a sheet of paper the words used in a committee meeting, listing the news and olds, the changes and intransigencies, the pluses and minuses. It comes closer to twentieth-century sympathetic magic than anything I know. Like all magic, it is thought to work most efficaciously where its effectiveness is not questioned or suspected.

So, if you are brave enough occasionally to raise stubborn questions about the realistic potency of these magic words, be prepared for some groans, for you may touch a tender spot. One need only ask "Does new mean good, in your view?" and the conversation is instantly set back to square one.

3

Defining Modernity

I use the term *modernity* in the same sense that many French people speak of *modernité* with a wave of the hand and upturned eyes, as something between "gauche" and "compulsive up-to-dateness." The Germans use the term *Modernität* in a similarly pejorative way.

Among the least functional habits of modern consciousness is the exaltation of the *modo*, the "just now," the most recent thing, as an unparalled virtue. This tendency is found even in the eighteenth-century definition of "modernist" as one who maintains the superiority of modern over ancient literature. It was long ago anticipated by the fourteenth-century debates about *via moderna*, the "modern way" of the nominalists who denied reality to universal concepts and paved the way for the disintegration of medieval scholasticism.

The modern habit, historically understood, is an old habit—centuries old. It is xenophobic toward past cultures. It fears past truth. It adores today, worships tomorrow, disavows yesterday, and loathes antiquity.

The most basic theological decisions one makes are often unnoticed, under the surface. At times they are quite unconscious. One only notices much later how crucial they were. One's inward attitude toward the assumptions of modernity is just such a fate-laden, consequential, unnoticed decision. Consciously or not, every believer must decide how much legitimacy he is willing to grant the assumptions of modernity, how deeply he will or will not allow himself to be intimidated by them, and how powerfully they will shape his perception of life in Christ.

Keep in mind that many Christians have existed prior to modernity, so surely it cannot be concluded that the assumptions of modernity are essential to or definitive for Christian faith. The harder question is to what extent the assumptions of modernity are even compatible with Christian faith, and if not, how the tension is to be lived out.

Modernity is less a time than a conceptual place, an ideological tone. It is less a distinct period than an attitude. Although it has had many premodern manifestations, it was not until the nineteenth century that it began to expand from the pockets of the intelligentsia into general circulation in Western society. By the twentieth century, moral attitudes that had been considered objectionable and disreputable in previous periods (due to classic moral arguments against abortion, sexual promiscuity, homosexuality, divorce, moral relativism, totalitarianism, and state dependency) had become the *Zeitgeist* of which the secular university came to consider itself the conscience and guide. By the last quarter of this century, the modern university had become less and less a *universitas* in the classical sense and more and more an exponent and apologist for the particular ideologies and mentality of modernity.

Characteristics of the Modern

The modern period may be used to describe the period since the French Revolution, or by some writers the period since the beginning of printing, about A.D. 1450, or some point in between such as Descartes or the idea of social contract.

The word *modern* is associated with a whole series of familiar English words rooted in the Latin roots *modernus* (of the present time) and *modus* (measure): Something is *modi*fied if it is changed, varied, or given a new form. A "mode" is a prevailing style or current fashion, as in dress, or a method or manner of existing. In metaphysics a mode is a way of being or form of something, as distinguished from its substance. One is "mod" who exhibits the characteristics of modernity. That is "modish" which is in the latest style, fashionable. A "modist" is a follower of fashion. A model is a style or design that is prone to change.

Consistent with all these nuances, that is *modern* which is characteristic of the present, or recent times, as opposed to traditional or ancient. Modern often points to tendencies in various fields, such as art, music, furniture, and literature. There is a pretense in modernity that what is not modern is not adequate, is antiquated, therefore to be thrown away.

The process called "modernization" implies that a society is undergoing a change from traditional to modern values, technology, or beliefs. There is an air of hubris about the term—it invariably assumes its own superiority. Some defenders of traditional societies in Africa and Asia feel that it is a short step from the overbearing claims of modernity to racism. The tendency toward arrogance in modernity is seen in Edward Shils' description that "Being modern is being 'advanced' . . . and 'rational'. . . . If such rationalizations were achieved, all traditions except the traditions of secularity, scientism, and hedonism would be overpowered" (Shils, *Tradition*, 288, 290; cf. Peter Berger and Brigitte Berger, *The Homeless Mind*, 1973; Peter Berger, *Facing Up to Modernity*, 1977).

Modernity is the effect of what Weber broadly called "rationalization" made possible by technology, bureaucracy, and a capitalistic market economy, and knowledge elites that give them ideas. The engineer, bureaucrat, entrepreneur, and professor have become agents of a modernity that clashes with traditional societies (Max Weber, *The Protestant Ethic and the Spirit of Capitalism*).

A Time, a Mentality, and a Malaise

If I insist on using the term *modernity*, the reader has a right to ask for a clearer definition of the particular way I am using it, even if it may be a definition that not everyone would agree on. There are three steps in my definition which, if missed by the reader, may render the remainder of my argument less clear in definition. *The term modernity has*

three distinct strata of meanings in this discussion, comparable to a target of three concentric circles with a bull's-eye.

(1) The outer, more general circle refers to modernity in
the wider sense of *the overarching intellectual ideology of a
historical period whose hegemony has lasted from the
French Revolution to the present.* It is a period whose key
general features (moral relativism, narcissistic hedonism,
naturalistic reductionism, and autonomous individualism)
have been well described by modern intellectual historians
(such as Peter Gay, Basil Willey, Crane Brinton, Herbert
Randall, Thomas Kuhn, and Paul Johnson), and whose
sociological features have been accurately delineated by
writers such as Max Weber, Robert Lifton, David Riesman,
Kenneth Boulding, Philip Slater, Erving Goffman, and Peter
Berger. These are descriptions of modernity that our discussion need not recount but importantly presupposes.

(2) The second, intermediate circle of our target defines
modernity more tightly as *a mentality, found especially
among certain intellectual elites, which assumes that chronologically recent ways of knowing the truth are self-evidently
superior to all premodern alternatives.* Religious thought of
the last two decades has been particularly susceptible to
taking its opinion with exaggerated seriousness, as if its
fantasies were self-evidently important to the future of all
humankind.

(3) The inner circle, or bull's-eye of our target, however, is
modernity in the sense of *a later-stage deterioration of both*
of the preceding viewpoints. It is a more recent rapid and
intense deterioration of modern consciousness. This deterioration has accelerated generally over the last half century but
in the last three decades has reached a dramatic moment of
precipitous moral decline.

It is only in the period since the mid-1960s that the bitter
fruits of modernity, which have been two centuries in
gestation, have been widely grasped, eaten, gorged, dis-
gorged, and found socially undigestible. This vomiting, on a
fairly large social scale, is an event of the last three decades.
The emetic has been sexual promiscuity, abortion, drug
abuse, and finally AIDS.

No simple schema can do justice to the rich complexities of
historical development, yet the function of a table is to

capture visually the most striking and evident categories of a problem for introductory clarification. It is with this hope that I attempt, in the table on pages 48–49, to sort out major differences between premodern, modern, and postmodern consciousness.

Some Revealing Features of Modern Consciousness

The rhetoric of unrestrained, individual freedom is a prominent earmark of the spirit of modernity. The goal of modern life is to be liberated from restrictions, constraints, traditions, and all social parenting—all of which are self-evidently presumed to be dehumanizing. "If we were only free from *x* or *y*," modernity fantasizes, "then we could truly be ourselves." This is a fantasy found as abundantly in the psychoanalytic theorists as in politics, modern theater, film, the arts, and popular culture.

The social, psychological, and political strategies and rhetoric of modernity all focus on a highly abstract notion of individual freedom. It is abstract because it is *taken away from (abs- + trahere)* its matrix of social accountability. The hunger of freedom to actualize itself quite individually is the despair of modernity, for authentic freedom exists only amid covenant responsibility. So the freedom for which modernity yearns is seldom responsible, listening freedom but a longing, self-negating "fallen" freedom that can only despairingly imagine itself to be free.

Sustained covenant accountability is misplaced in the interest of subjective self-expression. The social result is precisely the inordinate, hedonic self-assertiveness that classic Jewish and Christian ethics have always eschewed as the center of the human predicament, the *yetzer hara* (evil inclination). Its horrifying consequences are often not recognized until one discovers a polluted beach, the results of acid rain, upraised barricades for an incipient revolution, a raging epidemic, or an impending genocide. Then we belatedly get worried and wonder what could possibly have gone wrong. We could have been prepared by a clearer view of the history of sin.

Modernity is chiefly distinguished by a predisposed con-

	PREMODERN ERAS (Prior to Eighteenth century)	MODERNITY (Eighteenth, Nineteenth, and Twentieth centuries)	LATER-STAGE MODERNITY (Third quarter of Twentieth century)	POSTMODERNITY (Embryonic, awakening, preparing to enter the third millennium)
WESTERN HISTORICAL EXPERIENCE	The Western intellectual and cultural traditions from Judeo-Christian and Greco-Roman antiquity to the Enlightenment	Rise of autonomous individualism, demystification, secularization, naturalistic reductionism, scientific empiricism, historical criticism	Precipitous deterioration of social processes under tutelage of radical autonomous individualism, narcissistic hedonism, naturalistic reductionism	Hunger for means of social maintenance, continuity, parenting, intergenerational traditioning, historical awareness, freedom from the repressions of modernity

CHRISTIAN THEOLOGICAL TRADITION			
Patristic, medieval, and reformation theologies, all of which adhered to the doctrines of the seven ecumenical councils, the orthodox consensus of the first Christian millennium; = classical Christianity	Rise of pietism, religious individualism, theological liberalism, theologies of religious experience, scientific study of religion, social gospel, neoorthodoxy, fundamentalism, modern ecumenism, existentialism, and process theology; = classical Christian symbols modernized, reinterpreted, demythologized, psychologized	Accelerating hunger for acceptance by modernity; centerless accommodation to assumptions of modernity in rapidly deteriorating phase; = classical Christian language debased yet without awareness of debasement	The possibility of postmodern orthodoxy, having been immersed in the deteriorations of later stage modernity, now reawakened to the power and beauty of classical Christianity, seeking to incorporate the achievements of modernity into an ethos and intellectus that transcends modernity under the guidance of ancient ecumenical Christianity

tempt for premodern ideas, a vague boredom in the face of
the heroic struggles of primitive and historical human communities, a diffuse disrespect for the intellectual, social, and
moral achievements of previous periods. Some might object
that it is only to be expected of any period, and not modernity
only, that its egocentricity would tend toward disrespect of all
other social norms and intellectual ideas. This is disproved by
the awesome respect that some societies have shown for their
ancestor's traditions and for social structures and ideas prior
to them.

The key distinction between late modern and postmodern
consciousness hinges on attitudes toward *parenting*. Late
modern consciousness sees most social parenting as alienat-
ing by definition. Institutional structures are viewed as
inimical to individuated human freedom. No responsibility is
felt for the nurture of social continuities or multigenerational
moral tradition. The struggle is for individual autonomy
against social repression. Overweening hope is pinned on the
personal moral competence of the individual who is expected
single-handedly to reconstruct the human situation better
than any social tradition ever could have.

This is why the modern period generally expresses the
psychological quality of the *adolescent's* struggle against
oppressive parenting and historical wisdom of all sorts.
Surely every adolescent needs at times to struggle for his or
her own individual autonomy against parental dependencies,
but when this mentality becomes a total worldview, political
ethic, psychological strategy, and interpersonal posture, it
fails to understand the legitimate functions of tradition-maintenance and historical reasoning. Nothing is more characteristic of postmodern consciousness than the willingness to be
parented by historical reason and the wisdom of social
experience.

In sum, these are axial assumptions of later-stage, falling-
to-pieces modernity:

contempt for premodern wisdoms,

absolutized moral relativism,

the adolescent refusal of parenting,

idealization of autonomous individualism,

awed deference to reductionistic naturalism, and

scientific empiricism as the final court of appeal in truth questions.

This is a sketchy profile of the ideology of corrupted modernity, as I am using the term. It could easily be amplified any late afternoon about five o'clock by listening to the talk and music and interactions of the so-called happy hours of the bars and cocktail parties of modernity.

Modern history is turning out to be embarrassing precisely on the basis of its own optimistic axioms. Not some theory but actual modern *history* is what is killing the ideology of modernity. I need only mention Auschwitz, Mylai, Solzhenit-syn's *Gulag Archipelago*, *Hustler* magazine, the assault statistics in public schools, the juvenile suicide rate, or the cocaine babies. All these point to the depth of the failure of modern consciousness. While modernity continues blandly to teach us that we are moving ever upward and onward, the actual history of late modernity is increasingly brutal, barbarian, and malignant. We see unfolding before our eyes the troubled, conflicted alliance between an optimistic evolutionary progressivism and regressive forms of nativist narcissistic hedonism.

The Sellout

Why then do so many religious leaders persist in thinking that they have a winner in modernity? Because it has become a precious tradition to nurture an illusion. We have been deeply ensconced in the progressivist illusion that modernity *by definition* inevitably must be a winner. So we do not even hear the count when we are down.

The illusion itself has become a pampered tradition, guarded by institutional protections. The game requires that we put on blinders to prevent serious glimpses into premodern wisdoms that could challenge modern assumptions. We cannot learn from past failures and achievements because we have already predecided that we in our chronological "superiority" (later = better) have nothing of importance to learn from past societies and worldviews. This is reflected in the prevailing assumption that any textbook written more than

ten years ago *must* be out of date—a premise more useful for
physics than theology or ethics.

These oppressive tendencies have held mesmerizing power over the leadership bureaucracies to which religious
communities have looked wistfully for guidance in recent
years. It is just this progressivist illusion that postcritical
consciousness is no longer willing to abide.

Yet the courage to resist prevailing illusions cannot easily
emerge from within the very sphere in which these assumptions exert unquestioned authority. That sphere is what I am
calling *modernity.* Modernity is not just a time but a set of
passions, hopes, and ideas, a mentality that prevails in some
circles more than in others, and nowhere more than the
university, the primary agent of the ideology of modernity.

The Pendulum

The image of a moving pendulum may help us grasp the
way in which the Christian community is constantly seeking
an equilibrium of tradition and renewal. The direction of the
church's teaching is continuously swinging, as a huge pendulum would swing, between the two extreme apexes of
archaism and accommodationism. Since it swings through
lengthy historical epochs, where a single stroke might take
half a century, its motion is often imperceptible, especially to
those who have lost historical consciousness.

As it moves toward the rightward, conserving side, it tries
not to get so fixated archaically upon tradition that it cannot
behold contemporary challenges. When it approaches the
extreme right apex, the social intuition is to push away from
an introverted archaism.

When, over a period of decades, the archaism is temporarily overcome, the pendulum moves ever so slowly (not
abruptly as modern change-agent ideologies imagine) toward
the leftward accommodative side. Just when one might think
that it has moved too far, it touches the apex of extreme
cultural accommodation, and then slowly one feels the pull of
the community back toward its center of gravity, which is the
proclamation of God's steadfast love in Christ addressed to
ever-changing human environments.

Where are we today in terms of that analogy? I confess to having some broad hunches, but the passions and interests of the huncher always appear in his hunches, so they should be duly discounted. Here are my hunches: In the 1960s the knowledge elites had swung so far to a leftward fixation on change that there was a diffuse, gut-level cultural awareness in the 1970s and 1980s of the urgent need to find the way back to the center again. We are today only at the preliminary stages of a vast cultural movement back to the center, which from the left apex looks like a conserving motion. Those trained with liberal eyes see it as a rightward trend, a new puritanism in sex and a new conservatism in politics. Though it could be an ephemeral trend, my hunch is that it may take half a century to complete and it is only now halfway through its cycle.

Suppose we existed instead in a different historical period, such as the seventeenth century, in which classical Christianity had been fairly well assimilated and in fact had substantially ossified. Then Enlightenment Christianity might have made more historical sense. We would be putting our shoulders to the other side of the pendulum to move it leftward toward relevance and engagement with the world, resisting the rigidities that prevent an engagement with contemporaneity. But we do not live in such a period, and those who imagine we do are badly mistaken. Remember, our era is the one that made AIDS an epidemic, that invented "crack," and that pushed divorce statistics to new highs. Christianity does not now need to restate the rhetoric of homeless freedom, which is already overstated in our culture.

We are now struggling on the accommodative apex to understand our particular calling in discrete situations. If at times I may seem to push too hard toward the center, it is because the theological majority still happily proceeds as if their leftward apex were in fact the legitimate center. So in relation to them I may have to resort to rhetoric that itself may be momentarily excessive in order to respond realistically to a prevailing excess.

Although I have used the analogy of a pendulum, a lifeless mechanism, its intention is to refer to highly personal decisions, to a history of responsible freedom that moves intermittently between its two apexes in a dynamic rhythm, never coming to a stop. If a pendulum permanently stopped, it would be dysfunctional and meaningless. It is only useful when it is in motion, working with tension-filled polarities. And such is Christian teaching, existing as it does between tradition and renewal, between apostolicity and contemporaneity, between Word and world, a tension that will never end as long as the church is lodged in history.

Most Protestant congregations include worshipers whose basic cultural outlook is conservative, yet often mixed with liberal views. Other congregations may exhibit a characteristically liberal outlook, yet almost always with conservative voices to check the excesses.

Pastoral leadership must try to understand historically the dynamics that motivate both views. Each has its own psychological hungers, sociological assumptions, and ideological rationales. It is a perennial challenge to caring Christian faith to learn to participate empathically in the frustrations and anxieties of both. Sensitive pastoral care will try to resist the tendency to view one exclusively from the viewpoint of the other, or to exaggerate either tradition at the expense of renewal or renewal at the expense of tradition. Yet there are moments in the historical process when one needs greater emphasis than the other.

The Fixed Habits of Modernity

Long-time dwellers in universities have been so thoroughly habituated by modernity to see the world with historical blinders that they often cannot imagine that the hegemony of modernity could ever end or even be legitimately challenged. That lack of imagination is the despair of liberal education. Ironically, those *best* trained by modernity are *least* prepared for the consequences of modernity, and for the hazards of the postmodern future that are already hard upon us.

If we had not already been existing in a situation of excess, the temptations of excessive response would not be so great. But we should not be too surprised if seemingly exaggerated responses are temporarily required in order to effect the directional change that our analogy implies. Some polemical strength and toughness may be needed in order to unmask the moral impotence of the waning modernist momentum. What we have obviously missed in this pivotal moment of reversal is the practiced moral judgment of classical Christianity and the theological method of orthodox doctrinal definition, which we might well have been learning from the fourth-century Fathers or even from the thirteenth- or seventeenth-century Scholastics, had we remembered that they have been here before.

Once we begin to regain this balance, we hope we can then proceed to renew the tradition and attend to its relevant reinterpretation. But we cannot renew something we have not yet understood. We cannot expand a tradition we have never appropriated. So we must go back to the basics and learn from those most able to teach—the prophets, apostles, saints, and martyrs. We can especially learn from the ancient ecumenical consensualists whose only purpose was to articulate the mind of the believing church. It is best to listen to them speaking in their own language, unhedged by convenient rationalizations and unassisted by modern interpreters.

This continuing tension of pendular movement between polarities is intrinsic to the structure of Jewish and Christian social thought, for the God of Jewish and Christian celebration is involved in history. That necessarily implies a creative tension between the tradition and the changing shapes and sounds of ever-variable human cultures.

The development of doctrine does not imply amending the substance of doctrine in each new age. It does mean addressing the changing vitalities of each new historical situation with the original apostolic tradition. The perennial challenge of ministry is to learn to deal with this tension both imaginatively and faithfully, so as to neglect neither the authenticity of the tradition nor the actual conditions of the emergent world. This is a challenge that Irenaeus, Augustine, Nicholas of Cusa, Calvin, and Teresa of Avila all have shared in extremely varied historical settings.

Trajectory Shift as Divine Gift and Human Task

But am I describing a momentum that has already turned around or one that will depend on us to turn it around? On the whole, the culture is already in the preliminary stages of reversal, yet in some locales the reversal is totally unrecognized (this is especially true in the universities), while in other locales it is already beginning to be an accomplished fact.

The reversal of the pendulum's direction today is best understood both as a gift to be received and a task to be accomplished. The reversal is occuring by God's grace, but we at times are also called to help or to let it happen. It is occurring beyond our own specific personal individual spheres, but it addresses our personal spheres in its particular definiteness. The reversal occurs at the juncture of providence and human freedom, grace and volition, denying neither, affirming both.

The fact that current public opinion analysis may provide evidence to support the assertion that the direction is reversing brings along a secondary temptation: to conform to a new accommodation based merely on a conservatively revised assessment of popular momentum.

A vast reversal of consciousness is occurring in our culture that at times seems to have an inevitability of its own. But if we rest easily in this frame of mind and if everyone were to do likewise, then the momentum would soon hesitate. So there is an accompanying moral requirement to push and persuade and work in specific contexts to let or help the momentum reverse and to help others to see the reversal of the narcissistic, hedonic, individualistic tenor of our times.

There are moments when I may feel that the corrective is already in the air, already occurring, with or without my consent. That is just the context in which I may be called on in the next moment to exert particular courage within my own specific sphere of responsibility to alter the momentum, when "I must do it or no one else will." There may be times when the individual will feel in an exaggerated way that he or she is the only one concerned, as Elijah felt under the juniper tree on the way to Horeb.

There have been times when I have imagined, in demoralized moments, that I am the only theologian who has despaired as deeply as I have despaired over modernity and the only one who has grasped the radical hope of a postcritical Christian classicism—but that, of course, says much more

about me than about the actual situation. With closer attentiveness I have learned, as Elijah learned, that there still
remain "seven thousand in Israel, all who have not bent the
knee to Baal" (1 Kings 19:18).

4

Postcritical Orthodoxy

When a theologian forgets the distinction between heterodoxy and orthodoxy, it is roughly equivalent to a physician forgetting the difference between disease and health, or axe and scalpel, or a lawyer forgetting the difference between criminality and *corpus juris*. Yet it is just this distinction that theology has over the past two centuries of alleged progress systematically forgotten to make. A long chain of regrettable results has followed for pastoral care, biblical studies, preaching, Christian ethics, and the mission of the church.

The Tentative Classification of an Evolving Species

It may sound like hairsplitting, but I prefer to distinguish *modernity* from that which conservative Protestants used to call "modernism," in the sense of the application of modern critical-historical methods of the study of Scripture and tradition. There is nothing in the ensuing argument that rejects the wise use of historical criticism, even though I resist the fantasy that historical criticism will in itself be a vibrant source of spiritual renewal for Christianity. Nor do I precisely mean by modernity what Pope Pius X called "modernism" in *Pascenti Dominici Gregis* and *Lamentabili Sane* (1907) that is "an alliance between faith and false philosophy" arising from curiosity and "pride which rouses the spirit of disobedience and demands a compromise between authority and liberty" (*The Papal Encyclicals*, ed. Anne Fremantle, 197ff.). For, while Pius X viewed modernism essentially as a theological movement, I am speaking of modernity as a more general attitude of secular culture that prevails particularly among intellectuals and that recent theology has gone out of its way to accommodate and emulate.

My usage of the term *postmodern* is therefore best understood in light of the special, although not unique, way I am using the term *late modernity*, viewed as an ideology. The postmodern person has been through the best and the worst that modernity has to offer. The postmodern person is looking for something beyond modernity, some source of meaning and value that transcends the assumptions of modernity. Neck deep in the quicksands of modernity, the postmodern mind is now struggling to set itself free. Some of these postmoderns have happened onto classical Christianity and experienced themselves as having been suddenly lifted out of these quicksands onto firmer ground. They have then sought to understand the incredible energy and delivering power of Christianity, and, in the process of returning to the classical texts of ancient Christian tradition and Scripture, have begun to discover that the orthodox core of classical Christianity constitutes a powerful, viable critique of modern consciousness. Who are the postmodern orthodox? They are the hardy pilgrims who have set their feet on the path of reappropriating classical Christianity, having been through the rigors and hazards of the modern consciousness. Many of my students have set out on this pilgrimage. They are now inviting their theological teachers to join them.

It is useful here to make a basic distinction between two types of orthodoxy: *pre-* and *post*modern. Both are schooled in the same scriptural texts. Both celebrate the same Christ. But one has journeyed through and dwelt in modernity, while the other has not. Postmodern orthodoxy is distinctive not in its essential doctrine but in its historical experience. It has been deeply impacted by modern sociology, physics, psychology, and, more so, by modern history, which premodern orthodoxy has either avoided or by historical accident never had a chance to meet. Postmodern orthodoxy by definition must have undergone a deep immersion in modernity and its varied forms of criticism (Marxian, Nietzschean, and Freudian primarily), worked for it, hoped with it, clung to it, and been thoroughly instructed by it, yet finally has turned away from it in disillusionment, only to come upon classical Christianity as surprisingly more wise, realistic, resourceful, and creative than modernity itself.

The analogy is one of an estranged love affair. Premodern orthodoxy never fell in love with modernity or never came close enough to be enamored of it. Postmodern orthodoxy quite differently is on the rebound from a heavy, entangling affair that forever held out the most ecstatic promises but never delivered. If postmodern orthodoxy is a little gruff and cynical at times, it is because it has been burned by these broken promises. That is why it is *post*. It lives in the afterburn of lost idealisms.

Yet it is orthodox only in the most embryonic sense. It is only now beginning to discover a love more chaste and true than modernity. It is not in a cynical mood except when it bumps or scrapes its old wounds, the deep aches and hurts that it knows only time will heal. And yet as a young lover it remains awkward and ungainly in the presence of its beloved. It is not yet a suave, confident, experienced lover.

In fact, it remains a serious question for premodern orthodoxy as to whether postmodern orthodoxy should even be called *orthodox* at all, for it has so much to learn, so far to go on the way to becoming well instructed. It has not learned its Greek and Latin well. Its garb, music, and vernacular make it still look far more like modernity than orthodoxy to those who see it only from the vantage point of premodern orthodoxy. But postmoderns have had a rich series of experiences that premoderns have not had. They are able to see Christian truth refracted through these experiences in a way that precritical minds find offensive and impossible. Premoderns have never been dazzled by or yearned for modernity or become enmeshed in an involved engagement or snarled bond with it. They may have touched it artificially, but they were never engrossed in it or loyal to it. That is the mark of postmodern Christians. They have been in love and shared modernity's dreams and hopes, only later to experience a restlessness that eventually finds its rest only in the mercy of God that modernity thinks it can do without.

In this sense, much of the self-proclaimed orthodoxy we
see around us is out-and-out premodern. This is not to say it is
bad, but only that it lacks deep immersion in the modern
critical spirit, for good or ill. How does postcritical orthodoxy
look upon premodern orthodoxy? With quiet admiration for
its rigor and sometimes with wistfulness, aware that the pre-
Enlightenment theologies had mastered disciplines now
virtually lost. Yet they know that precritical orthodoxy will
not really do for the postcritical situation. Today we know full
well that it is up to us to reappropriate the ancient tradition *in*
the modern setting. No one can do it for us. So, however
much we may admire the tradition-maintenance of the Copts
and Amish or the pre-Emancipation Judaism of the eighteenth-century stetel, these cannot serve as direct paradigms
for the postmodern renewal of the Jewish-Christian tradition,
because they have so strictly barricaded themselves against
all forms of alluring intercourse with modernity.

Not so with postmoderns, who have already roamed widely
through and risked radical encounters with the therapies,
sciences, philosophical muddles, political strategies, and
aspirations of modernity, yet have not found there the buried
treasure that was advertised. They have plunged to the
depths of psychoanalysis, behavior modification, structuralist
sociology, relativity theory and quantum physics, existential
ethics, deconstructionism, Marxist politics, and alleged sexual
"liberations" of every kind, and yet have come away from
modernity more demoralized, only belatedly to discover that
the classical Jewish-Christian tradition is wiser and better,
more realistic and humane, than any of these.

Paul of Tarsus is an earlier prototype of the same pattern of
one who first underwent the full rigors of Pharisaic Judaism,
who earlier had opposed Christianity with all his might,
immersing himself completely in its opposition, only to
emerge out of this experience as Christianity's most eloquent
spokesman to those least inclined otherwise to understand it.
Orthodoxy has repeatedly learned that it is best defended and
understood by those who have once known and later re-
nounced false opinion. For it is precisely through attacking
the faith that one comes to see it from the outside in a relation
of special intensity and therefore is able to grasp it later from
the inside with a special intensity. The true faith is articu-

lated with best results, wrote Leo to Chalcedon, when heterodoxy is resisted by those who have understood it best by having had the direct experience of following the madness of apostasy, only later to perceive its inconsistency or pretense.

By analogy, those who have most deeply shared in the illusions of modernity may be best prepared to understand the complexities and depth of modernity's challenge to Christianity. If psychoanalysis, for example, constitutes a definitive challenge to Christian anthropology, how can one respond realistically unless one has first empathized sufficiently with psychoanalysis to grasp its challenge, which is not easily perceived by premodern consciousness?

My personal mentors in this journey have been a few characters seemingly born out of time—I mention particularly Will Herberg, Edwin Lewis, Joseph Mathews, and Albert Outler. For they all participated deeply, vigorously, and with life-involving commitments in radical politics and liberal hopes (Herberg with the Communist party, Lewis with the social gospel, Mathews with humanistic existentialism, and Outler with historical relativism); only later, having experienced the exaggerated promises and pretensions of modernity, did they turn to the pit from whence they were digged. Among earlier prototypes who anticipated postcritical classicism in profound ways I owe unending debts to John Henry Newman, Søren Kierkegaard, G. K. Chesterton, C. S. Lewis, and T. S. Eliot. But none of these can be said to be truly postmodern except in a highly provisional and anticipatory sense, because modernity had not yet played out its spectacular burst of disintegration in their lifetimes.

Neoorthodoxy: Why Did It Fail?

An understandable confusion that arises among some sophisticated audiences is the erroneous assumption that when we say orthodox we are really thinking of the neo-orthodoxy of Karl Barth and Reinhold Niebuhr. It is an understandable case of mistaken identity, and one that needs to be cleared up decisively. Neoorthodoxy, by no fault of its own, did not live deep enough into the outrageous decline of

the twentieth century to behold the precipitous moral deterioration of modernity. Barth and Paul Tillich in the 1920s
could see the cracks in the surface, but it was not until the
late 1960s that the structural nature of those cracks became
fully evident.

The major exponents of neoorthodoxy thought of themselves basically as reformist change-agents rather than con-
servators of ante-Nicene tradition. Compulsive reformism is a
spirit that runs directly counter both to pre- and postcritical
orthodoxy. Whatever differences they might have had among
them, all of them—from Emil Brunner to Anders Nygren,
from Friedrich Gogarten to Rudolf Bultmann—thought of
themselves as programmatic theologians essentially out to
alter the tradition rather than sustain, cultivate, or defend it.
Furthermore, neoorthodoxy on the whole was enormously
bored by liturgy, sacrament, pastoral care, concrete tasks of
ministry, spiritual formation, and the holiness of the church—
all issues with which we are now deeply engrossed. Most
major neoorthodox figures (notably Tillich, Barth, and Niebuhr) have been greatly enamored at times with messianic
socialist politics, a tempting habit that postmoderns, to the
man or woman, have found it necessary to kick.

Suppose we take Reinhold Niebuhr as a leading prototype
of neoorthodoxy, as many do, despite the fact that he himself
detested the term. How well does Niebuhr resonate with
what I am calling *postmodern orthodoxy*? Not very well. For
Niebuhr, it must be remembered, conducted an unrelenting
polemical campaign against what he called *orthodoxy*, from
his first book, *Does Civilization Need Religion?*, to his last
one, *Man's Nature and His Communities*. He consistently
viewed himself under a reformist self-image as one who was
battling to reverse the trend of a dated ecclesial tradition that
had become inextricably mired in social inequities and
bourgeois conservatism. Although postcritical students can
learn a great deal from Niebuhr about the criticism of
modernity, he would hardly have had much sympathy for
their fascination with the sociology of tradition-maintenance
or for their Chalcedonian Christology or trinitarianism. Niebuhr had more confidence in the moral resources of the lone
individual (note *Moral Man and Immoral Society*) than in the
wisdom of the social process, on which orthodoxy hangs its

theological method, and although he was a critic of extreme autonomous individualism, he never accurately estimated the depth of the gross interpersonal failures to which it would lead us.

If not Niebuhr, then suppose we take Barth as a prototype of neoorthodoxy. Barth cannot be termed postcritical in our sense because he never entered empathically enough into the ideological categories of modernity or the ethos of the late stages of deteriorating modernity. To the degree that he is orthodox, he is more premodern or intuitively antimodern than postmodern. Although once a low-keyed Harnack liberal, he never became grossly infatuated with the illusory dreams and fantasies of modernity which redounds to his credit, but this does not qualify him as postmodern, for postmoderns must be first burned by modernity before its successor can look plausible to them. Barth is one from whom we can still learn much, but it is only by some stretching that we could speak of him as postmodern in the strict sense.

If not Barth, then suppose we consider Bultmann as a type of neoorthodoxy. But Bultmann, more than any recent theologian, has focused on the accommodation of Christian language to modern categories, particularly to the existentialism of Heidegger, hoping to demythologize the Christian message in order to gear it into categories "acceptable to the modern mind." So the energies of Bultmann's project are flowing precisely in the opposite direction from the spirit of postcritical orthodoxy. And one must say the same even more forcefully of Tillich, who made a massive attempt to correlate and adapt Christian categories to the cultural assumptions and existential questions of modernity. Thus all the major representatives of neoorthodoxy fail to provide adequate models for postcritical orthodoxy, and it is best not to allow the two terms to be confused.

Without exception, the leading neoorthodox theologians thought of themselves as radical Protestants standing in protest against both liberal theology and classical orthodoxy. Therefore, it is only some decades later that we have a vantage point from which we may recognize or sense a slightly adolescent psychological tinge or quality in much of their writing, as they attempt desperately to break free from parental inputs, both liberal and orthodox. Postmodern orthodoxy, on the contrary, is intently concerned to listen carefully to these parenting inputs from within the frame of reference of having passed seriously through and beyond modernity. Nothing is more important to postmodern young people than good parenting. For they have beheld the consequences of so much bad parenting.

So there is a sense in which liberalism, neoorthodoxy, and fundamentalism are all surprisingly more like each other than any of them are like orthodoxy in tone and spirit. For, although they all had different responses to modernity, they are all more deeply enmeshed in the spirit of modernity than postmoderns, who have learned by many difficult routes that modernity is only a fleeting stage of human consciousness on which Christianity must not bet all its chips.

Rather than confusing postcritical orthodoxy with *neo*orthodoxy, I would rather view it oppositely as *paleo*orthodoxy. For it is seeking to *re*present the *old* orthodoxy in a credible way amid the actual conditions and broken symbol systems of the modern world. It is searching for its premodern roots, yet joyfully living before God within the frame of modern cultural pluralism. It is, in short, the very classical Christianity against which neoorthodoxy constantly struggled and by which neoorthodoxy was always frustrated and embarrassed.

Fundamentalism: Why Did It Never Try?

Another point must be sorted out for evangelical readers. None of the people I am describing as postcritically orthodox are properly categorized as "fundamentalist." Yet whenever the term *orthodoxy* surfaces, some mentally translate it as a synonym for a Scopes Trial type of fundamentalism which can so easily be caricatured as Bible-thumping. So to avoid this misplaced identity, it is necessary to show precisely how the postcritical recovery of ancient ecumenical orthodoxy differs from recent Protestant fundamentalism.

In pursuing this distinction, I do not want to offend evangelical or neo-evangelical colleagues by inaccurately pinning the label of *fundamentalism* on those who have long ago disavowed it. I realize that the worst habits of fundamentalism have already been broken by most neo-evangelical scholars, even though those changes have hardly been recognized in liberal circles, who still prefer to wield the word *fundamentalism* as a polemical club on a straw man. So it seems due time to identify the concept of fundamentalism historically with some accuracy in order to distinguish it from orthodoxy.

The five "fundamentals" of the Bible Conference at Niagara, 1895, offer a telling *selection* of doctrines as a nucleus for Christian thought: plenary inspiration of inerrant Scriptures, the Virgin Birth, the substitutionary theory of atonement, the bodily resurrection of Jesus, and the imminent second coming of Christ. If one reflects on it, the major premise of nineteenth-century historicism (that faith is based on historical facts and evidence) is much more determinative in the *selection* of these points than either patristic or Protestant scholastic orthodoxy.

Why are these five concerns more "fundamental" than others, such as divine providence, justification by faith through grace, or the triune God? What is the ordering principle of selection? Where is the church? The Holy Spirit? Sanctification? Sin? The principle of selection of these five fundamentals makes good sense only if seen in the context of a nineteenth-century historicism that was at that time influential but is now waning. Amid this then-rising historical spirit a determined effort was made to establish faith on the basis of objective historical evidence.

Why did the high estimation of objective historical evidence take on such importance, when it had caused relatively little flap previously? Because the nineteenth century had witnessed the powerful emergence of historical consciousness (Hegel, Darwin, Marx, Nietzsche, Spener, and so on) that expressed a consuming interest in historical origins and evidence. Despite its protests against this spirit, fundamentalism was inadvertently swept away by this modern historical consciousness and unwittingly became an instrument of it. Fundamentalism could not have happened in any century prior to the nineteenth. All this supports an ironic correlation: modern fundamentalism is more akin to liberalism than either one of them would be willing to admit. Both tacitly assumed that faith was based on objective historical evidence and both were overconfident of their forms of evidence.

Carefully note the chief presupposition of the turn-of-the-century fundamentalist program subtly conditioning its key questions and answers: that Christianity is best defended by historically establishing its objective factual origin. But this is the shared assumption of all nineteenth-century historicism. So it is not surprising that fundamentalism was far less interested in the doctrinal significance of the Resurrection than the fact of the Resurrection. It did not defend the doctrinal meaning or confessional import of the Virgin Birth nearly so vigorously as the fact of the Virgin Birth. This is consistent with the essential credo of historicism that faith is based on factual historical evidence. In affirming this credo, liberal historicism and fundamentalist historicism remain to this day very much alike.

Although it may on superficial view seem that fundamentalism was simply not modern enough, from a larger perspective the more subtle problem is that it was too modern in a quite surprising sense: namely, that it was too deeply trapped in a defensive and collusive reaction to modern historicism, preoccupied as it was more with faith's evidence than with faith's substance.

So it is confusing when we persist in thinking of recent American fundamentalism as an ancient or time-honored view or as identical with classical or patristic Christianity. Even though fundamentalism belongs collusively to modern historicism, however, it still cannot be thought of as postcritical in my sense because it never became sufficiently disillusioned with modernity, never risked a deep encounter with modernity's experimental edges, and never bottomed out on modernity's skid rows.

Those who have been involved in charismatic movements, either Catholic or Protestant, may wonder how the spirit I am describing as postcritical orthodoxy relates to their experience. The connection is this, as I see it: Those who have been powerfully moved by the Spirit are now being given an opportunity to learn more of the historical activity of the Spirit by which they are being moved. The Holy Spirit, after all, has a history. If charismatics focus only on the Spirit's present activity and forget the history of the Spirit's lively renewing activity in other times and places, they do not have a firm basis for discerning how the Spirit is moving in the present, or for discerning the difference between true and false doctrine. Not all charismatics are (or even wish to be) orthodox, nor are many of them postcritical in my sense. But many of the brightest and best of those whom I am describing as postcritical have been touched by and reintroduced to the central vitalities of the Christian tradition by these energetic communities, at least enough to set their feet on the path toward deepened historical awareness, clearer doctrinal definition, and a fuller engagement in Christ's mission to the world.

Embryonic Profile

I have been trying to distinguish postcritical orthodoxy as an embryonic theological type from neoorthodoxy, fundamentalism, earlier confessional Protestant scholasticism, and charismatic pietism. If it is none of these, strictly speaking, what is it? What does it amount to?

Some may in exasperation be tempted to say all that I am referring to is the traditional Catholic *magisterium* wrestling with deteriorating modern experience. Odd as it may sound, because this is largely written by and about and for Protestants, this definition is getting somewhat closer to descriptive accuracy, but even then it leaves much to be desired. For included within my definition of classical Christian orthodoxy are the Protestant theologies that adhered to the ecumenical patristic definitions. Although the thrust of this agenda will sound rather Catholic to free-church Protestants, it will still sound extremely Protestant to most Roman Catholics. In any event, it seems fair to say that postcritical Protestants are digging deeply into the patristic and medieval texts that Roman Catholics and Eastern Orthodox have always found edifying. So be it. A rich stratum of ecumenism has suddenly been reached. And all this quite apart from the expected channels of institutional ecumenicity! The agenda for ecumenical theology consists in probing this deep stratum to discover what has happened to us, why our roots in the same early tradition are more fundamental than our differences,

and why amid the challenges of modernity we need each
other more than ever.

Who are these "postcritical" individuals who view themselves as orthodox? Can we name any recognizable names?
Although this would surely help the reader with the identification of a gestalt, it is more difficult than it sounds
because its best representatives are still too young to have
written significantly. And even the major writers they are
reading, furthermore, often are not fully representative of the
type. It is easier to say who they are being influenced by than
to present a cast of characters for a fully developed "school"
at this early stage. They are much more drawn to historical
than contemporary figures. They are more likely to be found
reading Cyprian, Eusebius, Ambrose, or Jerome than Harvey
Cox, Sam Keen, Mary Daly, or Hans Küng. Among contemporary writers, the social scientists that are more likely to
intrigue them are the likes of Robert Nesbit, Philip Rieff,
Robert Heilbroner, Lewis Feuer, Seymour Lipset, and Peter
Berger. Among figures in psychology and pastoral care they
may be found reading James Dittes, Don Browning, David
Bakan, Thomas Szasz, Frank Lake, Paul Pruyser, Newton
Maloney, and Paul Vitz. In constructive theology they will
often resonate with Wolfhart Pannenberg, Helmut Thielicke,
Yves Congar, and Helmut Gollwitzer, and with American
writers like Avery Dulles, Herbert Richardson, Letty Russell,
and Paul Jewitt. They are likely to be found taking seriously
some political figures generally rejected by the knowledge
elite, such as George Gilder, Joseph Cardinal Ratzinger, and
Malcolm Muggeridge, and others like *Sojourners*, Jacques
Ellul, George Weigel, or Richard John Neuhaus on questions
of ethics and contemporary society. Among biblical scholars,
they will be found reading both European and American
writers who wish to utilize but not idolatrize the historical-
critical apparatus. Some are neo-evangelicals, but just as
many have come out of neoorthodox backgrounds, and others
are of Catholic tutelage; yet their views do not jibe slavishly
with any of these. They tend to be independent and imaginatively self-controlled thinkers. They remain as yet small in
number, and if they were all gathered together at an
American Academy of Religion meeting they would seem no
bigger than a distant cloud the size of a person's hand.

5

Voices of Postmodernity

The term *postmodern* was used systematically perhaps for the first time in 1971 by Ihab Hassan in relation to literature, and subsequently in the 1980s it made its way gradually into the social sciences and hermeneutics. It was not until after I had written on postmodern consciousness in *Agenda* that I began to realize that something remarkably similar was going on in architecture.

Postmodern Architecture as a Cultural Paradigm

In July of 1980, over a year after *Agenda* was first published, the Venice Biennale Exhibition launched its first international architecture exhibition, with a title that corresponded with my theme in *Agenda*: "the Presence of the Past." Its motto was "The End of Prohibition" (namely, the prohibition of beautiful classical ideas that had been damned by modernity). This exhibition became the symbol of post-modernism. It represented the "return of architecture to the womb of history." I was fascinated by these descriptions as analogies to the religious situation.

Postmodern architecture was putting "into circulation fragments and methods of the great historical tradition of the Western world that seemed filed away forever, and incompatible with the technological and theoretical conquests of our world" (Portoghesi, *Postmodern*, 1983, 6). "The word mod-

71

ern, originally designating continual change, has undergone a
process of sclerosis in identifying itself with a style, contami-
nated by the stasis of an unproductive situation" (ibid., 14). It
was an architecture seeking to respond to the "postmodern
condition" (Jean Francois Lyotard, *The Postmodern Condition: A Report on Knowledge*, [French ed., 1979]; Elie
Theofilakis, *Modernes, et apres?*, 1985).

Postmodern architecture represented "a refusal, a rupture,
a renouncement, much more than a simple change of direction," for "exactly what many of us do not want anymore
today is the antiquated Modern, that set of formulas which, in
the second decade of this century, acquired the rigidity and
clarity of a sort of statue," and whose "main article was
precisely an annihilation of tradition, the obligation toward
renewal, the theology for the new" (Portoghesi, 7). Postmodern architecture was making its way "toward the recovery of
certain aspects of tradition. . . . This recovery of memory, after
the forced amnesia of a half century, is manifest in customs,
dress (folk, casual, and the various revivals), in the mass
diffusion of an interest in history and its products" (ibid., 7).
These architects and artists "have discovered that the perpet-
ual invention of and search for the new at all costs" has been
toxic to urban humanity. Humanity is "not an animal to be
programmed in a laboratory, but an already existing species
which has almost reached maturity, while architects were still
trying to realize their obsolete project of modernity" (ibid.,
12).

Shortly after the Venice Biennale, the Polish labor union
Solidarity produced a document on modern architecture that
viewed the modern city as an alliance between bureaucracy
and totalitarianism. It viewed the break with historical
continuity as the great error of modern architecture.

The Modern Movement in architecture, seeking despairingly to change society for the better, viewed people as
objects to be rationally modified. This was carried out more
consistently in Soviet architecture than anywhere else. Architecture sought to make man modern, to coerce modernity
upon a populace, whether they wanted to see it or not. Today
this project seems colonialist and imperialist, vesting too
much power in state planners and regulators. But only a short
time ago modern architecture was viewed as salvific.

With the emergence of postmodernity, those who remain "guardians of modernity at any cost" have suddenly become the "new conservatives" who refused "to relinquish their privileges and power" (ibid., 8). The Modern Movement itself had inverted into "a real orthodoxy" with "fundamental dogmas," of which Portoghesi cites three: functionalism, antitraditionalism, and technologism. These are the dogmas that are undergoing criticism under the conditions of post-modernity.

Modern architecture, like the rest of modernity, has been left with a problem of legitimation, a lack of plausibility among those it has presumed to serve (Jean Francois Lyotard, *The Postmodern Condition*). The Modern Movement has been found to have "no more right to eternity than other movements" (Portoghesi, *Postmodern*, 32). "Under the pre-text of curing the world of its ills, they continue to propagandize old formulas whose ineffectiveness has already been extensively demonstrated." The Modern Movement "imposed on the entire world an unprecedented levelling" and "destruction" and "annihilation of archetypes," based on an ideology filled with "promises of salvation" (ibid., 32). This is the Modern Movement that had "decreed the annihilation of traditional architectural codes in the twenties." (ibid., 35)

Charles Jencks has described variables characterizing the differences between modern (1920–60), late modern (1960–), and postmodern (1980–) architecture. It is astonishing that they correspond so closely to the transitions currently being experienced in theology. Some of these characteristics may be summarized as follows:

Modern Architecture	Postmodern Architecture
utopian	popular
idealist	pluralist
Zeitgeist	tradition
purist	eclectic
antiornamental	ornamental
antirepresentational	representational
antimetaphor	prometaphor
anti-historical memory	pro-historical memory
antihumor	prohumor
antisymbolic	prosymbolic

"Alternative labels are hard to find" (Jencks, *The Language of Post-Modern Architecture*, 6). "Labels are convenient historical constructions. . . . To gain persuasive power, to command assent, they must refer to a complex nexus of identifiable ideas" (Jencks, *LMA*, 6). The labels we are currently using probably won't last long, but the reversal of consciousness has already decisively occurred.

Postmodern Aphorisms

Whatever outlasts modernity is postmodern.

If the modern simply means what is happening now, then there will continue to be ever-changing nows until the end of history. But something will follow what we call the modern period and the ethos of modernity. That may be called postmodern.

Modernity would have no way to end if it were an ultimate category. Yet modernity persists in the illusion that it is the ultimate, unsucceedable tradition.

The key to modernity is the notion of choice—choosing oneself, and choosing for oneself over against all traditional ways. The key to *hairesis* (root word for *heresy*) is the notion of choice—choosing for oneself, over against the apostolic tradition.

Modernity left a city without order in a state of civil war and mutual destruction. The partisans kept on changing the landmarks and street signs.

Modernity remains enamored with its own self-description. Modernity has never been as unique as it has commonly described itself to be.

Most social scientists, historians, critics, academics, and knowledge elitists have been ideological agents of modernization. They have maintained a debunking attitude toward traditional values and beliefs. They are the ones now on the defensive.

The simplistic distinction between modern and traditional is itself a prototypical modern idea.

Some people think that one who wishes to return to a traditional world merely extends the modern effort at self-creation. This is the way that modernity explains the return to tradition.

Social science interpretations of traditional/modern conflicts have tended presumptively (and I think inaccurately) to see the modernization process as irreversible. No trend in history is *ipso facto* irreversible.

Modernity may be described either as liberation from tradition or the loss of rootedness, depending upon one's moral sense. While the benefits of modernity may seem obvious to many, to others they seem increasingly doubtful. To those who view the benefits of modernity as obvious, the worst fear is traditionalism, with the specter of the loss of freedom that modernity has brought. To those who doubt that the benefits of modernity are obvious, the fear is the continued tyranny and unexamined power and hubris and overextension of modernity.

Modernity is experienced by some as liberating but with great costs, by others as liberating with low costs, and by others as binding and far too costly for its benefits. The latter is my view. Of what costs? The dissolution of the family, the loss of covenant sexuality, the breakdown of traditional values, the irretrievable loss of neighborhoods, the tyrannical imposition of new rules, the regulatory intrusion of government upon every aspect of private life, the loss of plausibility of religion, the loss of safe streets, the sense of homelessness in the world—modernity exacts unconscionable costs.

Modernity pretends that all futures are likely to reflect the assumptions of modernity. That in fact is one of the assumptions of modernity. Its advocates simply cannot imagine their own assumptions ever being transcended. This gives the odd pretense of permanence to the radical relativism and infinite mutability of modernity.

Modernity will never understand postmodernity because it is by definition committed to the defensive-conservative illusion that nothing will transcend modernity. Rather, "Modernization is always in a reciprocal relation with countermodernization—and has been from the beginning. There are oscillations in this relation, and at times one party to the dispute dominates, at times the other" (Berger, Berger, and Kellner, *Sociology Revisited,* hereafter SR, 149).

Modernity is from the viewpoint of classical Christianity

the amalgam of all modern heresies (*Lamentabili Sane*, 1907, *The Papal Encyclicals*, 202).

Postmoderns are those who refuse to take modernity as the final expression of providence in history. They are not intimidated by a period of history that is now waning. They refuse to accept modernity's descriptions of itself as an ultimate, irreversible, untranscendable stage of historical progress. They see modernity with its gifts and limitations as a relatively minor and passing episode in the long history of providence.

The Critique of Pure Modernity

Do I exaggerate? Writers on modernity often exaggerate the unified character of the modern period and the modern mentality. But the sin is a common one in historical inquiry. Such simplifications are virtually inevitable and necessary in any historical generalization or periodization. The alternative would be to regard history as a random set of events for which no generalizations are possible.

All attempted descriptions of modernity that I have seen have sinned by overgeneralization. But all descriptions of all historical periods that I have seen have so sinned. If one is to talk about historical periodization at all, one probably will soon commit this sin.

David Kolb has rightly pointed out that "Discussions of postmodernity presuppose that our age is unified enough that we can speak of its ending" (Kolb, *The Critique of Pure Modernity*, 262). Yet even Kolb continues to employ, for lack of a better category, the term *postmodern*.

An uncritical critique of modernity is one that shares the fundamental assumptions of modernity. Many recent attempts at "postmodern" criticism or hermeneutics or philosophy fall into this category. Kolb's *The Critique of Pure Modernity* (1986) is one such idealization of modernity. It lacks any real sense of the vulnerability of modernity and tends to perpetuate the illusion that modernity is immortal. The voices of Riesman and Ellul are regrettably missing in his analysis.

The 1979 discussion of postmodern orthodoxy that was developed in *Agenda for Theology* has been ignored by postmodern philosophers such as Lyotard, Theofilakis, Derrida, and Kolb. Why? The fact that I am avowedly orthodox is a sufficient reason for these writers to consider me as counter-postmodern. But that is just what remains at stake in this project—Can there be a postmodern orthodoxy? I think so. They think not. Their dogmatism itself is evidence that they are ultramodern, not postmodern. *Agenda* anteceded Lyotard, Kolb, Taylor, and the Foucault-Habermas debate, yet was never even slightly recognized as a part of their discussion. Nor did it deserve to be because it challenged the premise of their discussion.

Widely varied aesthetic, critical, and hermeneutical movements are now termed postmodern (see Richard Rorty, "Posties," *London Review of Books*, Sept. 3, 1987; Mark Taylor, *Erring: Postmodern Atheology; Religion and Postmodernity*). Much that pretends to be postmodern only rehearses the themes of modernity—the pretense of new creation, the hatred of tradition, the idolatry of self (Jacques Derrida, *Margins of Philosophy*). Jencks writes: "When I first wrote this book in 1975 and 1976 the word and concept of Post-Modernism had only been used, with any frequency, in literary criticism. Most perturbing, as I later realized, it has been used to mean 'Ultra-Modern,' referring to the extremist novels of William Burroughs and a philosophy of nihilism and anti-convention." Jencks used the term in an opposite way to refer to "the end of avant-garde extremism," and "the partial return to tradition" (Jencks, *The Language of Post-Modern Architecture*, 4th ed., 6).

Resistance to modernity has been consistently present throughout the many decades of modernity, especially in its earlier phases (with Reformation orthodoxy, the Counter-Reformation, and pietism). Until recently resistance to modernity has been countercultural. Today it is a flood tide.

Modernity's Compulsive Self-description

The despair of modernity is the thought that there are infinite possibilities open for self-actualization, that it is up to me alone to decide on who I am, to determine myself, to choose myself, to become myself. This mode of consciousness deserves clear description. Consider it like a neurosis being described by a caring physician, not a judgmental act of a prosecutor.

One becomes modern when one believes that one is becoming cut off from traditional values. This belief may persist even when one is in the process of passing along (or "traditioning") modern values. One enters the illusory stage of modernity the moment one has imagined that one has cast away the bondage of the past and the limitations imposed by traditional social roles. Hence feminism and Marxism and psychoanalysis are prototypical expressions of the modern illusion.

In describing modernity, I am less interested in following the methods of social scientists (Weber, Shils, Berger) and philosophers (Heidegger, Habermas, Kolb) in making this description than of working off common modes of awareness of modern persons, the kinds of consciousness that anyone in modernity would instantly recognize, like "I dread paying taxes," "The old neighborhood is now a parking lot," or "She's remarried, once again to a philanderer."

All periods of history have experienced their uniqueness—this is not to be denied any culture. But our form of modernity has felt that its uniqueness is more different from other societies than any before. We fancy that we are creating something entirely new in history. We moderns imagine that we are wholly unlike any previous period. We have accomplished this by doing away with antiquated traditions. We are not defined by traditions, as were all premodern societies. We are in the process of choosing ourselves, not allowing ourselves to be chosen by a traditionary process (Richard Palmer, "The Postmodernity of Heidegger," in *Martin Heidegger and the Question of Literature*, edited by William Spanos, 71–92).

This gives us the special illusion of being in control, being powerful, being masters of our destiny. The natural world appears to be given for our planning and manipulation and reordering (J. Habermas, "Modernity versus Postmodernity," *New German Critique* 22, Winter 1981, 3–14; "Habermas and Lyotard on Postmodernity," in *Habermas and Modernity*, edited by Richard Bernstein, 161–76).

We imagine ourselves as capable of infinite improvement.

Not only our societies but our internal feelings are reformable. Everything around me appears as changeable. Even I myself am infinitely changeable. Through therapy I can overcome all my past alienations and decide what I want to make of myself. "The modern expectation is that everything can be changed, that things could and probably should be different from what they have been" (Kolb, CPM 8).

There is no goal out there for me to attain, only what I decide. There is no purpose, only what I determine. There is no vocation for which I was intended, only what I want to do. This is modernity.

Antiparenting

Narcissism is a key mark of modernity. Myself becomes the central project of moral interest; self-enjoyment and self-development become the central goals. This is closely related to radical individualism. If other times attended to the parenting of a successor generation, in our period each one cares mostly about oneself and one's present happiness (Christopher Jencks, *The Culture of Narcissism*).

In modernity one discovers himself only by emancipation from traditional social roles. One undergoes psychoanalytic "therapy" to break away from parental and superego constraints and "become oneself," develop one's ego. Therapy does not return one to her family but gives her a pass. "The conception of the naked self, beyond institutions and roles, as the *ens realissimum* of human being, is the very heart of modernity" (Berger, Berger, and Kellner, *The Homeless Mind*, 213). It should not be surprising, therefore, that *"Modern societies are marked by a high degree of deinstitutionalization,"* which means "that modern social order is peculiarly unstable, unreliable, vulnerable to disintegration. Another way of putting this, perhaps in Paretian terms, is to say that modern society is prone to a peculiarly rapid form of decadence" (Berger, Berger, and Kellner, SR, 157).

Modern Western persons persist in assuming that their individualistic hedonism should be the self-evident goal of every society. This trajectory runs directly against the wishes and hopes of many non-Western cultures, who have the right to make their own adjustments between their traditions and modernity. The modern person views the traditional symbol as a disguise, a ruse, a mask to hide behind. This amounts to a systematic distortion of one's ability to listen to texts written by premodern persons.

The one thing I have learned in hermeneutics which has changed everything is what I can only call "obedience to the text"—listening to the text itself instead of modern interpreters of it. This was the most improbable and difficult and revolutionary thing that has ever happened to me intellectually.

What traditional societies viewed as legitimated values become for modernity merely descriptions of value. Norms are translated into descriptions of the norms of others. "Thou shalt keep the Sabbath holy" is translated into "This community believes in the norm that the Sabbath should be kept holy." The first statement is a moral norm. The second is a description that someone has a norm, with no normative judgment being applied. Ethical relativism assumes that there is no normative way to judge norms. One flees into the safety of describing norms held by others than oneself. This procedure amounts to a debunking of all norms (M. Foucault, *The Order of Things*: An Archeology of the Human Sciences).

Modern humanity is trapped in the maze of its own moral relativisms (Michael Galgan, *The Logic of Modernity*). God may enter the arena of modern conversation but only on the terms that God be accommodated to modern relativism and naturalism.

The Crisis of Modernity

"Modernity has entered a critical stage" and "this crisis is deepening" (Berger, Berger, and Kellner, SR, 147). Weber and Freud thought that if the individual's rational beliefs and actions became the basis of social construction they would be closer to the truth than traditional society, which provided the individual with identity, beliefs, and social roles before one ever made a decision. This premise is in crisis.

There is a curious antihistorical quality about modernity. Since modernity has transcended the past, it thinks it can dismiss it, or control it with repressive hermeneutics. Biblical historical criticism, when accommodative to the assumptions of modernity, is repressive hermeneutics, unwilling to allow the text to speak through the modern sieve.

The commonplace characterization that Islam is going "fundamentalist" is a particularly amusing generalization that reflects the ignorance of modern reporters. For *fundamentalism* is a word that has a peculiarly American Protestant history and is only imposed upon Islam with great awkwardness and predictable misunderstandings.

Moderns do not know what to do with emergent traditional movements the world over. The Welsh Nationalists look like troglodytes to a bemused press. The battle that continues in Northern Ireland seems completely absurd to pragmatic consciousness, but Irish consciousness continues to be pervaded by an engagement with its history. The melting pot has failed to cook away ethnic identities.

There remains a diffuse hunger for tradition in modern society, a phenomenon that modern categories cannot encompass. All ideas are plausible to modernity except the one that would make modernity dated (Edward Shils, *Tradition*).

It would be better if in social science the values of modernity would be treated in the same way as any other social phenomenon, as if modernity had "no privileged status as against its traditional or neo-traditional alternatives" (Berger, Berger, and Kellner, SR, 151). This is a moral imperative for social science, but one more often breached than followed. We would hope that social scientists might deliver to us their descriptive data unaffected by advocacy assumptions. But social scientists remain inveterate advocates of receding modernity (Thomas S. Kuhn, *The Structure of Scientific Revolutions*, 1970).

So we live, and will live out the rest of this century, amid the decadence of modernity. Decadence comes from the Latin *de* (from) and *cadere* (to fall)—it is a falling away from previous powers, a process of deterioration, a period of decline. If a cadence has rhythm, decadence has lost its rhythm. It has the same root as *decay*, i.e., to become rotten, to pass gradually from a sound to a deteriorating condition. Something is decaying if it is currently experiencing a precipitous decline of health, a tendency toward dissolution, a wasting away. Modernity is decaying (Karl Mannheim, *Diagnosis of Our Time*). This fall is analogous to the fall of humanity from its original condition as created.

I do not assert that the West is decaying (Spengler) or that capitalism is receding (Marx) or that America is decadent (Mailer). Rather, modernity as a period and a defensive ideology is decaying. Western capitalism and American democracy show every evidence of outliving modernity.

Decadent always modifies something, like the decadence of Rome or of the postwar expatriots. A decadent writer is one who writes in and about a period of decline. In this sense, modern writers are all inevitably decadent insofar as they imbibe the spirit of modernity, which itself is in a decadent stage.

INTERLUDE: CANDID TALK WITH OLD CO-CONSPIRATORS

Candor is an asset to conflicted communication. When I try to touch the essential energy and passion of this agenda, I envision a conversation not in a legislative hall but rather around a crackling fire with several good friends. The subject is "the future of theology," but at the moment we are deeply conflicted about it.

There are five participants in this conversation besides me, all old friends gathered to reminisce about our salad days and battle scars. They include a former Benedictine monk (Anthony); a social activist professional (Ted); a scholarly working pastor (Frank); Frank's daughter (Jane), whom I've known since her pigtail stage and with whom I have marched and sung in the civil rights movement, who has just completed her seminary education; and an evangelical black lay leader and adult teacher in an integrated church (Cassie).

It would take too long to set forth all stances in the conversation, but I will try at least to state the essential viewpoint I developed on that memorable evening, though not verbatim and salted with poetic license. I am not reporting an actual single conversation but a composite. The names are not the names of real people. Keep in mind the premise: I know my partners well enough to pull no punches; I care about them very much, but at the moment we experience a wrenching and awkward conflict.

The Ironies of Catholic-Protestant Dialogue

Tony had been waxing strong about Catholic charismatics, recalcitrant bishops, and his own earlier inner struggle with celibacy, when I found myself saying, even to my own surprise, that I was beginning to become aware of the loss Protestants have sustained in post–Vatican II Catholicism, which we all cheered as we watched it unfold. I remember how moving it was to me personally to be sitting there in St. Peter's Basilica while the debate was proceeding on *Gaudium et spes*. It softened my smugness, taught me how delicate the conciliar process can be, challenged my Protestant narrowness, and fired a wide-ranging new interest in ancient and modern Catholic consciousness. That was in 1965. Now a quarter century has passed, and I am still trying to assess the unintended aftermath of Vatican II for Protestants. I am amazed at how quickly all of our worst Protestant habits have become Catholic addictions.

"We are only now beginning to realize how much we as Protestants have relied on the stability of Catholicism to be there checking and constraining our experimentation," I told Tony. "We were free to do laboratory ecclesiology as long as you 'bloody papists' were there giving us a base out of which to be Protestants. After all, Protestantism began as a resounding protest, and you gave us something to protest against, and you have always *been there* for us to wrestle with and at times to quarrel with. For four hundred years we could count on you with your canon law, priesthood, and sacraments. We have always had you to fight.

"But now you are less and less that impregnable bulwark that gave us a certain point of reference. Now that you have faded into what seems to us like semi-Protestants and tardy liberals, we are beginning to miss the solidity of your ('our') tradition. Probably neither of us has realized how unconsciously we have depended on each other for the mutual correction of our wildest exaggerations. The acquiescence of

one pole of a tension that has lasted for four centuries has vast
and unexpected meaning for the other pole.

"At one level, it makes us angry; at another level, anxious.
For we are now forced to carry part of that traditionary load
you have always conscientiously carried for us. We are
densely ill prepared. You are still better equipped for the
tasks of tradition-maintenance, liturgical continuity, canonical
procedure, and moral definition, but growing less so by the
day. The only places we see you these days are where you are
leching about after our favorite old Protestant strumpets—
subjectivism, messianic idealism, emotive enthusiasm, and
ethical relativism. You have abandoned us paradoxically by
joining us!

"So there is a sense in which the developing Protestant
agenda for theology today must be a very Catholic agenda,
but no longer in the Vatican II sense—rather in the spirit of
the Counter-Reformation and Vatican I! We are for the first
time beginning to appreciate what was happening in the
period from the Council of Trent and Ignatius Loyola and
Melchior Cano through Carlos Borromeo and Roberto Bellarmine and Francesco de Suarez to Newman and the First
Vatican Council. [I could feel Tony's blood pressure rising.]
Essentially that period witnesses the attempt to conserve and
incorporate into the ancient tradition the challenge of nascent
modernity and the critique of Protestantism. It was characterized psychologically by a hunger for the delivered tradition
and sociologically by institutional maintenance and doctrinal
cohesion—exactly where the postmodern Protestant battle
line now lies.

"But, when my closest Catholic confidants discover that I
am thriving happily on the stockpiled resources of the very
period of theology from which they are now trying desperately to escape, they are alarmed at my shortsightedness, and I
am a bit stung, because I do not mean to upset them. They
become more vexed, however, when I show signs of uneasiness about the waves of reported new movements in Roman
Catholic theology, movements familiar to anyone who knows
beans about nineteenth-century Protestantism.

"I can understand, when I make an effort to be empathic,
how you might be fascinated to discover a Feuerbach, a
Rauschenbusch, or a Schleiermacher in new clothing. But I

dread all the ills that lie ahead of you on those paths. I have had several recent conversations of this sort with ardent postconciliar Catholic colleagues who are eagerly reading Johannes Metz, Ivan Illich, Leonardo Boff, Hans Küng, and the rest, some of whom sound like faint echoes of some combination of Harry Ward, A. J. Muste, Reinhold Niebuhr, Jürgen Moltmann, Richard Shaull, and R. M. Brown. When I risk becoming self-revealing, I realize that what they are doing makes me inwardly sad, and I suspect that more Protestants than will admit it are beginning to feel a strange sense of malaise about the rapid disintegration of Catholic authority. Will Catholics be able in four decades to commit every major mistake that took Protestant theology fully four centuries to make? The latest odds seem to favor it strongly."

Women and Excellence

Jane entered the conversation at this point with a pungent analogy: "What you are feeling about Roman Catholic renewal, Tom, I am feeling about the women's movement today." I asked her to help me see the analogy.

"That requires telling my story," she said, "but I'll spare you the long version. I have plunged in, lobbied for, celebrated, and sweated over the women's movement for years, since I read *The Feminine Mystique* as a teenager. Although I have always been resistant to the brassy, outraged, frenetic edge of the movement, I am now feeling a deep sense of pathos about it. It's becoming ever more entrapped in the competitive, materialistic, bourgeois syndrome against which it earlier had validly protested. I now feel a curious sadness that its idealisms, too, are being betrayed by self-interest and insensitivity. This betrayal is reflected in my own personal history.

"I bottomed out in the mid-1970s on a combination of consciousness-raising, social outrage, assertiveness training, and 'doing my own thing.' I followed these with the Zen trip, the Psi trip and the EST trip, only eventually to find my way back into my own Jewish-Christian tradition through the healing care and incredible love of a small group of genuine Christians whose lives were shaped by Acts 2:42 (sharing in the sacrament, praying, experiencing community, and following the teaching of the apostles). Now I am trying to see my own trial-and-error experience in relation to God's grace."

Jane asked me what I thought might be in store for committed Christians seriously engaged in advocacy of women's interests. "I distinguish between feminism and women's interests. Feminism has made too many misjudgments about women's interests to represent women generally. The idealization of outrage, the unisex myth, the link between feminism and lesbianism, and above all the identification of abortion with women's rights have lost feminism the high moral ground in the eyes of many women. Feminism is in significant part responsible for the feminization of poverty. The feminization of poverty did not occur without the sexual revolution, the readiness among women to go it alone, the desire of women for independent existence, the willingness of women to mate without monogamous marriage.

"I see Christian involvement in the women's movement in relation to its possibility—what it could be. Christianity is giving to the women's movement so little of its depth. Much of what passes for Christianity among feminists is only a tamed, faded, nineteenth-century religious optimism tinged with Marxist rhetoric and nativistic messianism. I am searching today not for a way to discount or abandon the women's movement but for a more complete fulfillment of it. This can only occur by better representation of women's interest. I hope in that process that it will be enriched by a Christian understanding of love, human tragedy, and divine mercy.

"Women urgently need the wisdom of classical Christianity, but thus far traditional Christian reflection has failed to reach out for young women with sufficient energy and empathy. Traditional Christianity has allowed itself to remain too much on the defensive in the presence of feminism. Only the Jewish-Christian understanding of sin can save feminism from its own self-deceptions and place its already keen awareness of human alienation in the context of divine providence." I asked Jane: "Where do you sense that the dialogue among Christian women may be moving?"

"Keep in mind that I have literally grown up with the feminist movement," said Jane, "motivated in part by political convictions. The liberal Protestant concern for social justice brought me initially into the movement and sharpened my commitment to it. I was reading Betty Friedan and Simone de Beauvoir in a church youth conference at sixteen. I have been elated by its achievements and have despaired over its inconsistencies. It is no unmixed blessing.

"What frightens me most is its willingness to build a political movement essentially on *private* self-assertion, often to the neglect of community and covenant bonding. What began as a warm, mutual concern for group support tends now to stress purely *individual* self-interest. What is needed is an extension of the women's movement beyond its present urban and upper middle-class elitism toward a greater populism and deeper moral awareness. Women must once again become the guardians of those inestimable values of social and familial continuity over which they have tradition-ally been the indispensable protectors. It is this potential extension of women's real interests that needs to stand in significant dialogue with Jewish and Christian scripture and historical wisdom."

It was out of this autobiographic context that Jane ad-dressed a poignant question to me: "To those of us who stand in this relation to the women's movement, it sometimes seems that we have no place to turn for wisdom in the dialogue between Christianity and fairness advocacy. Are we expected to make it up as we go?"

"My first hunch is that you would do well to invest as much time with texts of classical Christianity as with the strident modern writers who assume they have transcended them," I said. "You know well the modern tradition of equal rights advocacy from Elizabeth Cady Stanton to Simone de Beau-voir, Germaine Greer, Kate Millett, and Rosemary Ruether. You have already explored the heights and precipices of that literature. Now fairness requires giving equal time to women's voices in the classic Christian tradition—from Paula and Macrina to Phoebe Palmer, from Teresa of Avila to Mother Teresa. Let them say what they have to say to you in your postmodern situation. You need to get yourself out of the stifling trap of modern historical assumptions. I don't think you do yourself justice by limiting your significant reading to modern sources or to women's sources. As I urge men to read

Clare of Assisi, so I urge women to read Francis of Assisi. Spend your best intellectual energies in solid exegesis of Scripture, and with those historical church teachers whose passion was the proper grasping of the word of Scripture (like Irenaeus, John Chrysostom, Ambrose, Augustine, Dame Julian of Norwich, Calvin, and Catherine Adorno). You need not be intimidated by the fact that most of these sources were written by men.

"If you are asking what the mainstream oldline, old-boy network of Protestant theologians has to offer you, I am afraid that the honest answer is 'Far too little.' We ourselves are not deeply enough rooted in Scripture and tradition to meet the challenges at hand for men and women. The door is open for us to venture together.

"You might say we are on equal footing—equally ignorant of the Scripture and tradition that could make us whole. In *Works of Love*, Kierkegaard wrote that the deepest level of our equality is our equality as sinners before God's self-giving mercy. This love voluntarily becomes subordinate to the neighbor's need, loving the one we see. Men and women alike must relearn this form of subordination from Christ. Men cannot achieve it for women, and women cannot bestow it upon men. The proper theological beginning for dialogue on equality is the radical equality of our dependence upon God, the misery that we equally share when we deny that dependence, and the mystery of our salvation from sin without preference to human status."

Affirming this context, Jane wondered if I had any encouraging word for young women such as herself, who are venturing more and more toward service in ministry. I replied: "The irony of your struggle as a woman in ministry feels something like this to me: You will have to draw from the deepest spiritual wellsprings of the Jewish-Christian tradition in order to offset those distorted aspects of the tradition that have unfairly placed you in culturally subordinate roles. You must also see that subordination belongs to life in Christ for both males and females. This makes it even more imperative that you discover for yourself the classical meaning of sin and salvation in Christ, according to the faith once delivered to the saints, in order to overcome the plausible resistances in your own consciousness to an otherwise unjustifiable compromise with Christianity.

"You may find it exceedingly difficult to celebrate and enlarge the Christian tradition, while at the same time continuing to whittle away at the recalcitrant injustices of the tradition. These conditions will require you to become a more sensitive, sharper theologian and teacher than you otherwise might have been. This is precisely because you will have to discover plausible reasons resonating within the deeper recesses of the tradition to overcome the more obvious objections in your own consciousness to the inequities of the tradition as you know and interpret it. That is why I predict that an exceptionally high quality of theological brilliance and exegetical awareness will emerge among women in ministry as we head toward the third Christian millennium.

"But at a deeper level my heart wrenches for you. It is a lonely pioneering venture on which you may be setting yourself. It is as though you were setting out on a long journey without any road maps. Who knows what will lie ahead? Surely you will feel the support of the community and your closest friends in crises, but when rejections abound, when alienations persist, when ugly inequities block your path, when others will not be able to understand you, will you be tough and courageous enough to persist and continue to grow through these adversities? There was a time, not long ago, when we could make pleasant promises to candidates for ministry of job security, minimum salaries, accoutrements, and splendid visions of upward mobility. Whether these expectations were a valid reflection of the essential tasks of ministry then is a debatable question, but in any case there is now grave doubt about how deliverable these promises may be in the future. What if very troublesome days should be ahead for the religious communities and for ministry? If the road ahead should turn out to be suffering, threats, possible imprisonment, and *marturia*, as I think some of it is likely to be, do we have a right to expect heroism and perseverance from women in ministry? Yes, of course we do. We will see it happen. But it should not be entered into lightly or with flags waving or with heady rhetoric or as a supposed means of upward mobility, but rather with realism and prayer."

The Black Experience and Evangelical Christianity

Cassie wisely pointed to the wide differences between the black theologians holed up in universities and the black ministers whose theology is more powerfully shaped by a living community of worship. The black tradition of evangelical preaching, he argued, is a richer context for theology than the modern university. I agreed, and this gave me the opener to say something to Cassie I had been wanting to say for a long time.

"For now you possess the precious gift of high moral credibility for your leadership and teaching. Use that gift wisely and prudently, without assuming that it will always be readily available. It is in part a legitimate compensatory response for long-standing injustices, a psychological attempt to redress the grievances of centuries. But it is not to your interest to bet on its absolute durability. It can vanish in a moment, depending on the shifting interest of the partner in interaction. Beware of those who promise that everything you say counts double. If you play into that collusion, both parties will later have to pay for it twice over in frustration and disillusioned hopes.

"Part of the scandal of classical Christianity for you, as for Jane, is that it comes to you delivered by the very Western culture that has in fact been a source of miserable oppression for your people. There is in all Jewish and Christian experience a scandal of particularity, that God meets us through special histories that reveal larger dimensions of meaning in universal history. The irony of your black American Christian tradition is that the message of spiritual freedom in Jesus was transmitted to you through a culture that robbed freedom, plundered dignity, and scarred deeply. But as has happened so many times before when the treasure of the gospel was carried in earthen vessels (wicked and unjust cultures), your church tradition was wonderfully able to sort out wheat from chaff.

"It remains on your theological agenda to make more sense biblically of these deep-going ironies. In taking up that task, you are not alone. Other peoples, such as the Jews and Armenians, Ukrainians and Cambodians, have faced genocidal threats, and many more have endured humiliating slavery for long periods of time only later to recover their human dignity and historic identity, notably the Greeks, the Irish, and the Slavs. Your struggle to understand your history as Christians rightly should be seen alongside these other genocidally threatened histories of dispossessed peoples. Jesus himself came as a poor man from a foreign-occupied nation. And it was none other than the apostle James who pensively asked: 'Listen, my friends. Has not God chosen those who are poor in the eyes of the world to be rich in faith and to inherit the kingdom he has promised to those who love him?' " (James 2:5).

I tried to express to Cassie my hope that he would not be so mesmérized by the alluring ideologies of modernity that he forgot his own black history of alienation or failed to see it in the light of God's own suffering for us. "My prayer is that your suffering will be illumined by the suffering of Christ for you and will bestow significance on the suffering we all from time to time face and are called to meet courageously. A crucial effort in the emerging theological agenda must be a pastoral theodicy that is learning to think theologically about and deal pastorally with those inevitable concomitants of human freedom: anxiety and guilt. If Kierkegaard was right, suffering and its meaning remains the toughest issue of our daily human existence. Christianity addresses a word to us about our suffering that transforms both our understanding of our suffering and the existing situation in which we experience suffering. It recounts how God suffers for and with us. Those who have more intensely experienced social alienation, who know suffering not merely as a concept but as a part of their daily walk, are far better prepared to understand and proclaim the gospel of God's suffering love than are the self-satisfied and hedonically satiated.

"This is why the black Protestant tradition has been so abundant in supplying vital energy to other Christian traditions. Black music has taught us to dance and sing the blues, but these teachings have not come without tears and suffering. Much black gospel music, even in its secularizing forms, has exceptional authenticity for us because we know intuitively that it has been hammered out of profound sufferings transmuted by faith. The moral credibility you now possess, and to which our conscience gives assent, has been hard won.

What I fear is that you might be easily outpromised by the immediatist messianic illusions of modernity so as to imagine that you can quickly transcend, through political rhetoric or psychological stratagems, the fundamental paradox and tension that characterize suffering human existence."

I implored Cassie not to let himself get trapped in the role of a victim by allowing others to view him essentially as dependent and therefore as having lost his inner dignity and initiative. "This is far too much to grant, and if you do it you will spend most of your time in interactions trying to correct its imbalances, even though you may momentarily seem to benefit from the generous, nurturant promises of the partner in the protector role."

Working Pastor as Theologian

Meanwhile, Frank had been weaving in and out of these conversations, and although his part will not be reported in detail, the gist of his concern throughout was the failure of academic theology to be of much help to the working pastor in his complex locus of responsibilities and crises. Frank, I might say, is an excellent pastor, the kind whose preaching many benefit from week after week because they know it corresponds with his existence as a person. What's more, he is a sensitive counselor and an astute spiritual leader of a fairly large urban congregation. In my view, he fulfills the teaching office of ministry in a magnificent way in his parish. That made his question come to me with even more force. He essentially was asking me, "When are you and other theologians going to develop forms of exegesis and theology that I can translate meaningfully into my daily parish ministry?"

I answered with another question: "When are you going to show us how theological reasoning can emerge concretely out of your own actual experience of ministry? We in academic theology must learn from you," I said to Frank. "We cannot any longer pretend that our highest duty is to import the next wave of theology from European universities or revolutionary political movements until finally it may filter down from the seminaries and clergy retreats to the local pastor and congregation. The flow must move exactly in the opposite direction, like a great tree drawing up nourishment and water from its roots.

"Only where the living tradition is being embodied by an actual community is theology working rightly. It is only out of the matrix of a credible embodiment of Christian community that excellent theology emerges. That is the territory of the pastor. That is where the wisest theological intuitions of the coming decades will be formed. I have the hunch that the next move in theology may be up to you, Frank, and others like you, rather than we in the academic centers who have systematically forgotten how to think theologically out of a living community of worship and service. This is a model for theology that we might have learned from Cyprian, Athanasius, Calvin, or Hooker.

"The neglect by academic theology of the essential subject matter of theology—God's Word to humanity—might be compared to the situation that would prevail if lawyers were to forget about trying cases in the courts and instead turn to the study of the literary analysis and aesthetic critique of court opinions. When ministers ignore the body of theology and church teaching in favor of other 'more relevant' disciplines and 'more interesting' bodies of knowledge—often the most ephemeral pop therapies and fad politics—a reversal is due. Such a situation is comparable to law teachers who would ignore the history of case law or heart surgeons who would leave the hospital and become preoccupied instead with the heart as a literary symbol of inwardness. Just as lawyers belong in courts and surgeons in hospitals, so ministers belong in the gathered worshiping community, gathered to facilitate its scattering into the world with renewed spiritual understanding. Our tradition of jurisprudence is alive where evidence is being examined by due process, where juries are sorting out the facts, and where judges are determining which law shall apply. Similarly, the religious tradition is alive where the religious community is remembering and celebrating divine grace, where the Word is faithfully preached and the sacraments fittingly received.

"Recently," I chided Frank, "I think you have been giving up on solid theological nourishment, largely because you perceive that theology has given up on you. Only a few years ago, you were reading theology avidly. How long has it been since you have carefully exegeted a Greek text or read a classical theological treatise or worked deeply, intellectually through a tough pastoral-theological perplexity? My guess is that you have read two books on psychology for every theological work you have read in the past ten years. Why? One principal reason is that many theological writers have not been even slightly interested in really addressing your dilemmas, much less listening to you. They have been on a different upward mobility pattern, trying to gain credentials in the university community with colleagues who by and large think that what you are doing is dull or naive. But you have also colluded with the faddists who have offered easy answers to the human dilemma by your granting them premature credence and not asking them the hard questions that come out of your daily ministry.

"Some of the most important periods of the history of theology have not been dominated by the academic theologians holding university positions (though Abelard, Thomas Aquinas, Melanchthon, and Schleiermacher represent this strand). Rather, there have been several key periods of theological development when the most pivotal insights have come from persons quietly engaged in daily ministry. This is particularly true of the first five centuries of the church's life, with great pastoral figures such as Ignatius, Polycarp, Irenaeus, Ambrose, and Augustine, but it is also seen in the tradition of George Herbert, Isaac Barrow, Philipp Jakob Spener, Richard Baxter, and John Fletcher, and right into the modern period with such powerful figures as Walter Rauschenbusch, Reinhold Niebuhr, and Martin Luther King, Jr. What would the history of theology have been without these key persons engaged in their theological reflection directly out of their actual ministries? It strikes me that we are entering just such a period today. Academic theology has played itself out or disavowed its texts to such an extreme degree that the immediate future of theology may literally depend on the exegetical and doctrinal insight of persons in daily ministries of Word and sacrament.

"If we focus on the early centuries of the church's existence, we find it difficult to think of a single major theological voice that was not in the pastoral office, serving daily as *episkopos* or *presbuteros* in a teaching ministry

accountable to an actual pastoral setting. Today we errone-
ously assume that anyone who is pastor of a congregation or
administrative leader of the church could not possibly have
time to do significant, sustained theological work. But not so
in the first half of the church's historical existence. During the
first millennium, it would have been unthinkable for anyone
to regard himself as a Christian theologian unless serving
daily in the pastoral teaching office. The university theologian is a late-appearing character in the Christian tradition. In
the early centuries, doctrinal definition was seldom done by
'professional' nonpastoral theologians, but rather by practicing liturgists, preachers, and pastors engaged in the care of
souls. Some such corrective is required today."

The Moral Crisis of Social Activism

Alongside these conversations, another more volatile one
had been brewing with my old social activist confrere Ted,
who stands in the best tradition of William Lloyd Garrison,
Elizabeth Cady Stanton, A. J. Muste, the Berrigans, and
Camilo Torres. He frankly expressed his horror at my fixation
on suffering, my fascination with Counter-Reformation Catholic thought and tradition-maintenance, and the excessive
confidence I am inclined to show toward the average pastor.
He wondered aloud if I have sold out completely on my
commitment to a politically active and relevant theology. He
himself is ordained but no longer maintains an active relation
with his church judicatory.

Ted inhabits a bureaucratic agency office in Manhattan that
towers over the Hudson River, from which he can glimpse the
huddled masses and the working poor. Although he despairs
over all institutionalized religion, no one is more trapped in it
professionally than he, who works daily as a liaison between
church agencies and government officials.

Ours is an old friendship that candor could never spoil.
Having listened carefully to him unload on me, however, I
felt that it was time for me to level with him about some of my
long-held feelings of uneasiness about his inconsistencies
and chronic self-deceptions. This turned out to be the most
painful exchange of the evening because our comradeship

goes back so far. But, hoping that our relationship might be tested in a different way and reconstructed on a better foundation, I confronted him with a long chain of questions, complaints, and grievances. These took on a momentum of their own and unfortunately became somewhat overstated, but they seemed contextually necessary in order to redefine where we were in our opposite trajectories. Even though my words now seem excessively harsh, I think it is best to express them as frankly as I did that evening in order to reveal the deeper emotive energy of this discussion as promised. My side of the conversation ran something as follows.

"How unconvincing is your talk of justice and poverty when you remain in your protected environment with guarded entry points and doormen who keep track of all intruders! There you sit with your executive washroom key, Yale Club identification, and travel budget, where you can talk a good game of oppression but you seldom meet the suffering poor or hear their voices or touch their hands or look into their faces. You have not shared in the lives of the oppressed except at a very safe distance. You live riskless in a comfortable house, so don't pretend to play the role of martyr. You have benefited from an education that you call liberal but that remains prejudiced against every historical period except your own. Aren't you, after all, the one from whom we have heard so much talk about how our ideas must correspond with our actions and how any religious vision may be dismissed if it does not have pragmatic results? It is you from whom we have heard that talk, yet your own life is a silent protest against the way you have been protesting.

"By now I feel that I know you pretty well. I have watched you inwardly delight in the death of the cherished values of your mother and father's generation—their hopes, their moral investments, their institutions. Like watching a lead demolition ball swinging from a highly leveraged crane hitting the walls of stately old buildings, you have enjoyed watching the collapse of carefully constructed institutions, bridges, fortifications, customs, and patterns of behavior that have been centuries in the making. You have shrugged and winked as the ball hit the colonnades, the old tapestries, the façades, and the support structures.

"You enlist the language of the prophets. And it is true that the God of Hosea, Isaiah, and James inspired you to a social conception of sin and justice, to ethical claims implicit in religious awareness, and to a vision of universal social reconciliation. You have blurred that vision, and the religious communities for which you are responsible are in deep trouble.

"While you have talked *Realpolitik*, Ted, you have apparently remained satisfied with passing resolutions and forgetting about them, and more so about those whose welfare your resolutions presume to protect. You have played the role of protector of the defenseless, yet haven't you made their lives a little the worse by overpromising and failing to deliver? You express grave concern over the environment and the economy, yet you burn boatloads of fuel in your two automobiles and airplane trips to convention centers where you imagine you are serving church and society by again revising organizational charts and tinkering with institutional machinery, often with the hidden interest of maintaining your own prestige and power."

"The meetings are necessary to bring people together to strategize," Ted replied. "And no institutions are being destroyed by our work—they are falling of their own weight."

"Face it," I replied, "the church has probably declined as quickly under the brief period of our own current leadership as it has under some of its most bungling leaders in its most disreputable periods of history. Can you name any historical period in which a generation inherited a religious community with more vitality and left it more demoralized? Our generation has accommodated thoughtlessly to the spirit of modernity and imagined we were doing the church a grand service by forgetting its historic understandings. Wherever this accommodationist influence has been greatest, the religious communities have most quickly deteriorated. Meanwhile, you have not been listening to the complaint of your own conscience because your therapist has been trying to help you feel less guilty. In fact, emotional health has become defined as the absence of guilt feelings of any kind, and your diluted theology has colluded disastrously by acquiescing to that definition. Incredible. It is hard to believe that such things can happen to such well-intentioned people, but it is just your assumption that your good intentions are inevitably reliable that has taken you furthest off course."

At that moment I received a deep look of recognition from Ted, born out of many shared experiences. Gently he said: "Tell me what you want. What are you asking of those of us who, like you yourself, have invested ourselves in a lifelong search for a socially responsible, politically relevant Christian ethic?"

Instantly I felt that it was much easier to state my critique than to point toward a constructive way ahead for Ted, for others, or even for me. But aware that his question pierced to a deep center that could not be artfully dodged, I took a deep breath and tried to respond: "What I hope would come from you, as from myself, is not a cheap reduction of the tension between the Christian ethic and political repentance, but an increase of that tension. I am not looking for a quietism that would cynically give up on a Christian political ethic, but for a more realistic political engagement rooted in an awareness of the depths of sin and grace. I am asking neither for a return to culture Protestantism nor to an overly simplistic dogmatism, but to a deeper critique of modernity rooted in Scripture's grasp of God's providence amid alienated human history. That means less self-deceptive idealism and more disciplined love in search of a social policy."

Although I am reporting only one side of this conversation, because this is a "viewpoint" essay, one can well imagine that the conversation had another side and that it was not without its own merits. The two-way dialogue that ensued was able to correct some of the exaggerations of my own outburst, but the purpose of this report is merely to get at the central energies underlying this discussion, and I think they are revealed as well in that rough-and-tumble eruption as anywhere.

That is the substance of what happened as I experienced it and responded to it—a one-sided report that surely could have been expanded to five times this length if equal time were invoked. Ted, my oldest friend among the group, was particularly stung and hurt at the depth of my outrage. What is ahead for our friendship is yet to be determined, but I felt that it was a good sign when, as he left, he pensively put his hand on my shoulder, looked me straight in the eye, and said: "Old friend, you are like the airline pilot who, fed up with the noise and crush and movement of civilization, decided to enter a Trappist monastery for a life of silence. The first day he was inspired and elated. The second day he became somewhat uncomfortable. The third day he was going bananas. By the fourth day, he stood up in the refectory and addressed his brothers: 'Brothers, it is time that we talk over this dubious rule of silence.' Hushed indignantly and carried away feet first, he shouted as he was tossed out by the main gate: 'Now is the time, if there ever was a time, to talk over and express ourselves fully about these oppressive rules of silence!'"

Ted, knowing me longest and best, had spotted my weakness. "Does that mean that I am as impatient with myself as I am with others," I said, "or that I have a low tolerance for follow-through, or that I am probably not personally ready for the kind of theological effort that I am challenging others to tackle?"

"Take your pick." Ted winked.

"Thanks, Ted," I said, "I need some time to worry about that." But I knew instantly how right he was.

Since that memorable evening, these items may be fully reported: Jane is now serving with distinction as an administrative assistant to a pastor in a large congregation where she is currently working with a small group studying Sister Macrina's teaching as reported by Gregory of Nyssa (*On the Soul and the Resurrection*, NPNF 2 V, 428–70). Ted's budget was cut and his church agency drastically downsized, but he was offered and accepted an attractive state government agency position. Frank has become an elder statesman among young pastors in his city. His latest letter indicated that he has still been unable to locate a copy of Gregory the Great's treatise on pastoral care. Cassie writes that his adult church school class is now studying Jeremiah with powerful consequence. And Anthony's marriage to the petite blond psychologist with whom he had planned to start an experimental "New Age" holistic growth center has ended in an amicable separation.

PART TWO:

THE CRITIQUE OF CRITICISM

The biblical historical criticism that has pretended to be an objective investigation of the history of Jesus has often turned out to be a highly biased account that imposed the values of nineteenth- and twentieth-century naturalistic reductionism upon the New Testament texts. Jesus Christ has been reduced to human hopes, aspirations, myths, class interests, and social influences.

Modernity demanded that the history of Jesus be submitted to all the canons of interpretation prevailing in alienated modern consciousness. Jesus was refabricated, remade into a political or social or psychological advocate. His words were squeezed, massaged, and reshaped into correspondence with the interpreter's current viewpoint.

Modernity has required that Jesus himself bear the cross of modern historicism, be scourged with the whips of feminist outrage, be crucified by modern barbarianism, and buried under piles of hedonic individualism and me-first narcissism.

6

Endgames

The Theandric Person and History

Historical inquiry into Jesus has not yet rigorously begun in our time. It will not begin until the premise of theandric union—that Jesus is truly God and truly human—is taken as a serious hypothesis by exegetes.

The notion so prevalent in the early church that novelty is proof of error has been reversed in modern times by the conviction that novelty is proof of truth. One who thinks this way will likely conclude its correlate: that premodern ideas are intrinsically prone to error precisely because of their antiquity.

An endgame, in chess, is the part of the game that continues after the decisive move has been made. Throughout the endgame it is certain that the decisive move will eventuate in a victory. But a number of moves, sometimes extremely complicated, remain before the victory is consummated.

Such is the condition of deteriorating modernity. The era is over. Yet a number of moves remain before it will be clear to all that the era is over.

The end of historical science as we have come to know it is an example of a small endgame going on within the larger endgame of decadent modernity. The players in the game are called criticism and the criticism of criticism. Criticism has seemed to be winning for two centuries. But a decisive move has been made—the application of the methods of criticism to criticism itself. The hermeneutic of suspicion is now being applied to the hermeneut himself—the class analysis to the analyst.

Historical Science amid the Endgames of Modernity

Many supposedly new procedures of modern historical inquiry were developed long before modern times. They are not entirely, as is often claimed, recent achievements. Yet modern chauvinism has encouraged the pretense that presumably new procedures and allegedly new discoveries about Jesus have made all previous testimony about him virtually worthless. These pretenses, the deft brilliance of some modern interpreters, and the massive appearance of the modern evidentiary apparatus have all conspired to make it easy for contemporary students to miss the stubborn limits of the critical method and its burdensome philosophical baggage.

Life has been given to us in this twentieth, not some other, century. We can be deeply grateful for much in modernity. But the modern hubris that assumes that it has finally discovered the true nature of religion is surely not modernity's strength.

Those who point to the gross pretensions of modern chauvinism do well to be wary of an equally regrettable attitude of undiscriminating adherence to anything and everything that emerges out of ancient, patristic Christianity. There is no good reason to reject modernity in an undiscriminating way, but rather only its pretensions, self-deceptions, and myopia. There is no reason uncritically to accept all ancient Christian texts in an undiscriminating way. Rather those texts that best express consensually the mind of the believing church surely deserve our renewed diligent attention.

The End of Modernity

Modernity is over, fully corrupted by its own premises. We are now in a postmodern period wherein the assumptions of modernity are no longer credible apart from a tiny group of introverted elites. Within this situation, we are challenged to reappropriate a classic critique of modernity, without cynicism and with charity toward all.

There is no cause either to despair or rejoice over the demise of modernity. The fact of its demise is an unheralded gift. The gift implies a new challenge amid a history that continually unfolds ever-new challenges.

Premodern orthodoxy studied Jesus Christ earnestly, dogmatically, and piously, but lacked certain critical-historical data and methods needed to inquire into the transmission of the tradition about him. *Modern biblical criticism* studied the history of Jesus historically, but with strong, often reductive naturalistic philosophical assumptions and predispositions. This is a cycle that appears to have come to an end (Maier, *The End of the Historical-Critical Method*, hereafter EHCM; Stuhlmacher, *Historical Criticism and the Theological Interpretation of Scripture*, hereafter HCTIS, 20–61). *Postcritical, postmodern orthodoxy*, having been disillusioned by the illusions of modernity, now seeks to teach the apostolic faith amid the rapid deteriorations of modernity. It is no longer intimidated by a failed modern consciousness by which recent criticism has been uncritically cowed.

Premodern orthodoxy approached the study of the history of Jesus with overweening *systematic-doctrinal* predispositions. Modern critical studies approached the study of the history of Jesus with overweening *naturalistic philosophical* assumptions. Postmodern orthodoxy seeks to approach the history of Jesus on the ground of *classic, consensual, ecumenic wisdom*, seeking to reformulate classical exegesis in the awareness of the broad failure of contemporary criticism to develop a viable, preachable, missional Christianity.

To premodern orthodoxy, historical debates tended to turn on predisposing *dogmatic* issues. During the hegemony of modern critical studies, doctrinal questions tended to pivot on *historical* issues. Now that modernity is essentially spent, postmodern orthodoxy seeks once again to ground church teaching in the *actual history of Jesus*, viewed as unique theandric person. Postmodern orthodoxy is "post" because it emerges out of the failure and demise of modernity. It is orthodox insofar as it hungers and thirsts for rigorous instruction from classical ecumenical Christianity.

Premodern orthodoxy sought to state the faith once for all delivered to the saints, based upon Jesus Christ of the canon. The modern critical spirit sought to recover the history of Jesus, yet in its endgame phase it has resulted in the virtual loss of any possibility of knowing Jesus historically. The malaise of historical-critical inquiry has resulted doctrinally in the tyranny of historical reductionism, setting the stage for postcritical orthodoxy, which celebrates renewed sustained companionship with ancient Christian teachers.

Though not rejecting precritical efforts, postmodern orthodoxy seeks intentionally to be postcritical. It approaches canonical Scripture with cautious, constrained, spare use (not rejection) of historical criticism, form criticism, redactive criticism, and source criticism. One may be greatly indebted to some aspects of Rudolf Bultmann's work, yet poignantly aware of the bone-dry valley into which his form criticism has lately shepherded preaching.

The patristic stones the modern builders rejected must now become the major blocks for rebuilding upon the Chief Cornerstone, the unique theandric person, Jesus Christ. The very apostolic teachers and classical exegetes that moderns have long assumed to be discredited have become indispensable postmodern, postcritical mentors. The best hypothesis for making systematic sense of the texts of apostolic testimony is the simple classic premise that Jesus is truly human and truly God in personal union (the theandric premise of John 1:1–18; Rom. 1:3–4; Mark 14:61–62, and other New Testament references).

Intentions and Results

Historical biblical criticism in its predominant forms, synchronous with the rest of overextended modernity, is coming to an end. There is a noticeable difference between the vast intentions and the slender results of historical biblical criticism. It was once widely thought that criticism would make the sacred texts more understandable, more accessible, more morally decisive. The ethos in which those views were held was called modernity.

(1) *Have the texts been made more understandable?* Historical criticism, which sought to enable a new engagement with the texts, in practice has inculcated a detached neutrality that has made it virtually impossible to respond to the text. Beginning with the intention to allow the text to speak, it has ended by inadvertently blocking the capacity of the text to speak. The aim was to make texts understandable to the modern intellect. The result has been the discrediting of the sacred texts among elites who imagine themselves to have outgrown the cosmological assumptions in which the texts were assumed to be imprisoned. Criticism, wrote Hans Küng, has tried comically to be "more Biblical than the Bible, more New Testamently than the New Testament, more evangelical than the Gospel, and even more Pauline than Paul" (EHCM, 45).

(2) *Have the texts been made more accessible?* Intending to make the texts more accessible to the culture generally, biblical historical criticism has fallen "prey to a form of technologism which regards as legitimate only those questions which its methods can answer." Intending to be radically open to human questioning, criticism's "objective neutrality" required "a sacrifice of the very questions the Bible seeks to answer." Meanwhile the alleged "objective standpoint" turned out to be "none other than the historically conditioned place where *we* happen to be standing" (Wink, *The Bible in Human Transformation*, hereafter BHT, 8, 3). The "we" refers to academics whose modern philosophical assumptions are being swallowed by the swift postmodern Leviathan.

Historical criticism has not merely knocked on our door. It has come to dwell in our house, intending a long stay. Its goal is "the intellectual mastery of history and the emancipation from all inhibiting tradition. But as such this cannot be the aim of a church whose very identity stands or falls by its connection with Holy Scripture" (Stuhlmacher, HCTIS, 62).

(3) *Has critical method elicited or inhibited moral decision?* Intending to enable radical moral decision, criticism has crippled decision by its anal-retentive fixation upon data collection. In the name of existential decision making,

criticism has undermined decision making. Karl Mannheim rightly grasped that "He who makes no decisions has no questions to raise and is not even able to formulate a tentative hypothesis which enables him to set a problem and to search history for its answer" (*Ideology and Utopia*, 89). According to Wink, "The outcome of biblical studies in the academy is a trained incapacity to deal with the real problems of actual living persons in their daily lives" (Wink, BHT, 6–8; cf. Irenaeus, Ag. Her., II.26, *Ante-Nicene Fathers*, hereafter ANF, I, 397, 398).

Under such circumstances one is reminded of Matthew Prior's line:

> Cured yesterday of my disease, I died last night of my physician (*The Remedy Worse Than the Disease*).

The whole spectacle is a little like "people who set their own house on fire" or "put swords in the hand of . . . enemies" or "disavow their own parents, taking them for strangers," who have "collected all that is frivolous . . . into one torrent" (Gregory Nazianzen, Orat., XXVII.6, 9, Ag. Eunomians, *Nicene and Post-Nicene Fathers* [hereafter NPNF], 2 VII, 287, 288).

7

The Broken Promise of Critical Method

The term "historical-critical method" includes a wide variety of methods in the study of Scriptures. Form criticism (*Formkritik*) has sought to lay bare the forms of oral traditioning that antecede the written text. Content criticism (*Sachkritik*) has applied critical judgment to what the text substantially says, especially as to what is judged meaningful to the modern reader, often restating the contextual meaning in contemporary idioms. Redaction criticism (*Redactionsgeschichte*) has sought to identify how various documents were reworked in relation to emergent cultural needs or challenges, especially with a view to identifying the theological tendency of the editor. Source criticism (*Quellenkritik*) has sought to identify the written sources used in the writing of the Gospels. Tradition criticism (*Traditionsgeschichte*) has studied the oral traditions that impacted upon written documents and the process of traditioning itself. Audience criticism has studied the various audiences to which a text or saying is addressed. Canon criticism has studied the process by which the Scripture became consensually defined and accepted. Text criticism has sought to identify the most reliable available text among various manuscripts.

All of these may be generally described as historical criticism in the sense that the methods, analytical procedures, linguistic tools, and resources of post-Enlightenment historical science were energetically applied to the study of the documents of Christian Scripture and tradition. Most of the critical methods noted have analogues and embryonic antecedents in classical Christian exegetes (especially Origen, Irenaeus, Athanasius, Gregory of Nyssa, Jerome, and Augustine). There is nothing wrong or evil about these methods as such, but only about their recent ideological captivity and biased application.

Critical method often is taken to refer only to those modes of inquiry that have developed since H. W. Reimarus (1694–1768), J. S. Semler (1725–91), and G. E. Lessing (1729–81). But that definition always errs in the direction of an unconscious modern chauvinism—the premise that modernity is superior to all premodern wisdoms. For critical-historical inquiry antedates modernity by over a millennium. Critical method was born out of classical Christianity. After languishing through many centuries of medieval scholasticism, it was belatedly revived in the Renaissance.

Insofar as it pits modern methods of inquiry against all ancient wisdoms, modern critical method displays an egocentric ideological bias against all forms of premodern consciousness. Such truncated criticism is best called not criticism but simply prejudice. It is a reductionist criticism that imports the philosophical assumptions of naturalistic reductionism as the central feature of the study of Scripture and tradition. Although critical method is often contrasted with dogmatic or systematic method, there is no adequate reason why they must necessarily be opposed (Schleiermacher, *Brief Outline*, 19–24; A. Schlatter, *Zur Theologie des Neuen Testaments und zur Dogmatik*, ed. U. Luck, 213; *Doc. Vat. II, 111–28*). Systematics without excellent criticism is vulnerably grounded; criticism without systematic reflection is sporadic, occasional.

When Kierkegaard wrote openly against "Christendom" (the prevailing culture Protestantism of Denmark), the "Christendom" appears in quotation marks to indicate a merely pretended Christendom. A similar bracketing is pertinent whenever postcritical theology speaks of "criticism," for it is pointing largely to a pretended criticism, hoping for and seeking a more profound criticism (for a thoughtful preliminary attempt, see P. Stuhlmacher, HCTIS, 61–92). This would require a post-"modern" or post-"critical" method. That shift has not yet been made, but is pending. To the praying community, it is a matter for petition, not thanksgiving. This study cannot at this point be diverted into a tedious investigation of the investigators or a suspicious inquiry directed against the modern form of the hermeneutic of suspicion. That needs to be done elsewhere, not here (for a start see Althaus, Stuhlmacher, and Meier; cf. Hans-Georg Gadamer, *Truth and Method* and *Philosophical Hermeneutics*; P. Ricoeur, *Interpretation Theory*, and *Hermeneutics and the Human Sciences*; J. B. Thompson, *Critical Hermeneutics*).

In its post-1960s forms, amid accelerating deteriorations of modernity, reductionist criticism has revealed its deepest edges of hubris. Scripture criticism is more firmly captive today to its modern (naturalistic, narcissistic, individualistic) *Zeitgeist* than Augustinianism ever was to Platonism or Thomism to Aristotelianism. Trapped in modern prejudices against premodern forms of consciousness, reductionistic exegesis has proven to be just as prone to speculation as were the extremest forms of Gnosticism, and as uncritical of its own presuppositions as supralapsarian Protestant scholasticism.

Thereby the legitimate services that historical criticism rightly should render have become lost or misplaced. Its credibility has been undermined by exaggerations and implausible hypotheses. Reductionist critics have become unbridled speculators unaware that they are speculating.

In English we use the phrase "the gospel truth" to mean that which has been reported with total accuracy and is beyond question as to its authenticity. Yet in the hands of historical critical method, the Gospel from which this phrase derives its power is viewed as a systematic distortion of the truth in the interest of early Christian preaching in non-Palestinian settings. The truth of the Gospel now has to be sought, it seems, by weeding out most of the actual language of the received documents, searching for the slenderest vestiges of supposed *logia* grudgingly imagined to represent early layers of oral tradition. There is an understandable limit to the tolerance of the worshiping community for such belabored speculations. Form criticism is a case in point.

Form Criticism and the Criterion of Dissimilarity

Form criticism has rightly assumed that the traditioning process occurs by oral transmission through certain predictable stylized literary forms, such as epigrammatical sayings, teachings, and myths (M. Dibelius, *From Tradition to Gospel*). Yet this assumption has tended toward speculative excess. We first illustrate by analogy to psychoanalysis and then by the use of a specific procedure—the application of the criterion of dissimilarity.

(1) *Form criticism as psychoanalysis of the text.* There is a disturbing analogy between form criticism and psychoanalysis. Both seek to unpeel embedded layers of alleged unconscious influences. The psychoanalyst seeks to uncover hidden, unconscious influences in a living client. The form critic is trying to uncover hidden influences in the written text of which the author was likely unaware. Both are highly speculative, yet prone to being unaware of their speculative excesses and prone to give their own methods too much benefit of the doubt, thus tending toward self-deception.

In making their interpretations, psychoanalysts rely upon a theory that alleges to be scientific, but whose scientific status is dubious. Form critics also seem to be doing scientific work, yet their science is little more than intuitive guessing based on tiny shreds of ephemeral, selective evidence. Both form criticism and psychoanalysis have become ossified into a hardened orthodoxy protected by fees and/or tenure and an elaborate apparatus of professional impression-management which has become deeply ensconced in departmental bureaucracies of German and American universities for over half a century.

(2) *The criterion of dissimilarity.* The more self-assured the form critics are the more they are fond of this curious assumption: that if any notion may be found in the history-of-religions environment available to Jesus, then it must not be his own words, but ascribed to him by another. A simple question vexes the reader: Does not this foreclose the possibility that Jesus himself might have innovatively utilized available symbols and concepts in a way fitting to his mission?

The criterion of dissimilarity has assumed that only those

sayings of Jesus are authentic which have no parallel in Judaism or in the Hellenistic church. Wherever such parallels are found, the form critics have routinely assumed that such sayings emerged not from Jesus but from some later adaptation of available cultural sources in Judaism or Hellenism (K. Koch, *Growth of the Biblical Tradition: The Form Critical Method*).

By this procedure form critics have proposed, in three phases, to eliminate as inauthentic those passages from the earliest synoptic materials. These are: (a) if an alleged saying of Jesus can be identified in contemporary Jewish sources, it presumably cannot be regarded as an authentic saying of Jesus; (b) other materials are eliminated because later post-Resurrection materials have allegedly found their way back into the accounts of Jesus' earthly ministry, hence they cannot be viewed as authentic; and (c) other materials are eliminated if a similarity can be shown with Palestinian Christianity (H. Conzelmann, *Religion in Gegenwart und Geschichte*, III, 623; G. Ebeling, *The Nature of Faith*, 52ff.; Marxsen, BC, 15ff.; E. Fuchs, *Studies of the Historical Jesus*; D. B. A. Calvert, *New Testament Studies* [1972], 18, 211ff.).

The little that remains—only scraps—are grudgingly regarded as "authentic" on the basis of the so-called criterion of dissimilarity, i.e., they are dissimilar to rabbinic, post-Resurrection, and later Palestinian phrases (Bultmann, *Theology of the New Testament*; R. H. Fuller, *The Foundation of New Testament Christology*, 243ff.; for a more balanced view see V. Taylor, *The Formation of the Gospel Tradition*). According to form critical criteria, a saying would be considered authentic only *if*: it is dissimilar from Jewish or Hellenistic traditions; it demonstrably has an Aramaic or Palestinian root; or it has some clear evidence of being grounded in the pre-Easter context.

Note that our courts of law require a different standard: innocent until proved guilty. The opposite is practiced by the form critics: "The basic premise is that the Gospels are untrustworthy as historical documents until proven otherwise" (Ramm, *Evangelical Christology*, 159). If one followed a similar procedure with Lincoln's Gettysburg Address, one would eliminate as inauthentic any references in the speech to concepts that could be shown to antecede the battle.

Such a procedure seems designed primarily to discredit a document rather than interpret or understand it. It would be like beginning to read Sophocles by saying: Anything Sophocles says he says will be credited provided he makes no reference to any terms in any antecedent document. Or reading Shakespeare with this presupposition: Anytime he uses a phrase that can be found somewhere else, we will assume that Shakespeare did not write it. Hence—since Shakespeare used the language common to all Elizabethans—such a criterion would be the basis for arguing that all of Shakespeare's works, like all other works (politely excepting the form critics', of course), were plagiarized.

In ordinary speech, however, people do not limit their choice of words to those that only they uniquely possess. Rather, they use words generally available to a culture. *This norm makes the fantastic demand on the text that it have no parallels.* Conspicuously, the form critics do not place that requirement on their own writings (cf. H. Riesenfeld, *The Gospel Tradition and Its Beginnings: Limits to Form Criticism,* 7–30; W. Kuemmel, *Journal of Religion* 49 [1969], 60).

The New Testament was largely written in an Aramaic- and Greek-speaking world. One who preaches and writes in Greek must use Greek words—words that have a long history, varied nuances, and multiple associations, which are variably put to work in proclamation. Yet these word parallels are not strictly speaking the source of the events or ideas reported in the New Testament but only the verbal channels by which those events and ideas are proclaimed. The critics have tried to explain the New Testament against its cultural backgrounds—not a bad thing to do—but in the meantime the gospel has become reduced to its linguistic, cultural, sociological, and political backgrounds.

Marxsen argues blatantly that Jesus, not the canon, is the norm of proclamation, but it is the Jesus he chooses by the method he chooses to use to find him. "Christology has to do, not with the exegesis of the New Testament texts as they now stand, but with material prior to the present form of the New Testament." He of course reserves the right to discount or eliminate redactive sources which do not "necessarily coincide with what the gospel writers intend to say" (Marxsen, BC, 4).

Under such circumstances, "Since each theologian conceives of the canon in the canon differently, and since this is done on the basis of an assumption no longer questioned (i.e., by free choice), uncontrolled subjectivity has the last word concerning what should have divine authority" (Maier, EHCM, 47).

A harsh value judgment is imposed by the form critics: the tradition supposed to be earlier is judged authentic, the later invariably inauthentic. This judgment has been covertly shaped by a long-standing Protestant prejudice against the catholicizing tendency that appears already in many New Testament writings. It is this predisposition that needs to be reexamined. The same issue was faced in Marcionism. Marcion had found an analogous pseudo-critical way of cutting out portions of the received canon and regarding them as "inauthentic." Tertullian thought that Marcion had the audacious "hardihood of blotting out the original records [of the history] of Christ, that His flesh may lose the proofs of its reality" (*On the Flesh of Christ*, 2, ANF, III, 522).

The form critics want to emphasize the less mature period of development of the New Testament canon and rule out the more mature and reflective development. This can be portrayed in this chronological sequence:

Oral Tradition	Paul	Synoptic Gospels	Hebrews Pastorals John	End of NT Period	Depositum Complete, Canon Formed

At the beginning of this process was the earliest Palestinian *kerygma* in oral form. At the end of this process were the New Testament documents that became canonized Scripture. The form critics increasingly distrust each successive stage, the later being least trustworthy, while the most trustworthy is what they conceive as the earliest stages. Stated more circumspectly, they trust only their own judgments and speculations about what went into that first stage. It appears to be a hermeneutical system whose rules favor the interpreter and disfavor the text.

According to classical exegesis, the earlier phases of development were a fully adequate *depositum* that needed later phases to explicate and develop key themes that were intrinsically embedded even in the earliest proclamation (cf. Vincent of Lérins, *Commonitory*; and J. H. Newman's principle that religious knowledge is more likely to be obscured than advanced by the lapse of time, *Parochial and Plain Sermons*, VII, 249; and that doctrines remain implicit till they are contravened, and only then do they become stated in explicit form, *Via Media*, I, 223).

The "Authentic Sayings"

Even if one takes such a constricted procedure seriously and reduces the sayings of Jesus to those that conform to the supposed criterion of dissimilarity, still surprisingly a great deal can be said about Jesus. Here are some of the remaining "scraps," passages to which the historicist's imprimatur has generally been given as passing the criterion:

Jesus understands himself as one who "[drives] out demons by the finger of God," and if so, "then the kingdom of God has come to you" (Luke 11:20 NIV). He speaks of himself as the bridegroom for whom the guests do not fast while he is with them (Mark 2:19). The kingdom he proclaims is like new wine bursting old wineskins (Mark 2:22). The coming heavenly feast is not limited to the people of Israel alone: "I say to you that many will come from the east and the west, and will take their places at the feast with Abraham, Isaac and Jacob in the kingdom of heaven" (Matt. 8:11 NIV). He calls hearers to not resist one who is evil, give the cloak, walk the second mile (Matt. 5:39–41). "Let the dead bury their own dead, but you go and proclaim the kingdom of God" (Luke 9:60 NIV). "Anyone who will not receive the kingdom of God like a little child will never enter it" (Mark 10:15 NIV). The way is narrow (Matt. 7:13). "How hard it is for the rich to enter the kingdom of God!" (Mark 10:23 NIV). "No one who puts his hand to the plow and looks back is fit for service in the kingdom of God" (Luke 9:62 NIV). "Everyone who exalts himself will be humbled, and he who humbles himself will be exalted" (Luke 14:11 NIV).

He tells the parables of the lost sheep (Matt. 18:12–13), the Prodigal Son (Luke 15:11–32), the hidden treasure and the pearl (Matt. 13:44–46), the unmerciful servant (Matt. 18:23–

33), the sower (Mark 4:3–9), the growing seed (Mark 4:26–29), the mustard seed (Mark 4:30–32), the Good Samaritan (Luke 10:29–37), the lost coin (Luke 15:8–10), and the Pharisee and tax collector (Luke 18:9–14). He exists in a special relation to God the Father, whom he calls "Abba," and to whom he prays, "hallowed be your name, your kingdom come" (Luke 11:2 NIV).

These sayings are generally judged "authentic" even by the form critics. The refreshing irony that continues to be ignored by the form critics is worth savoring: If ecumenical Christianity had a canon limited only to these sayings, there would still remain the rudiments of classic Christian teaching—triunity and theandric union in the person of Christ.

Is Jesus' Self-Understanding Knowable?

Is it necessary to saving faith to establish with absolute certainty the precise view Jesus had of himself?

This raises the larger question of whether anyone's self-understanding can be certainly or objectively known. To ask whether we know what view Jesus took of himself is something like asking whether we can know through exhaustive study what view Julius Caesar or Freud took of himself. Note all the squabbles over psychohistory. It is considerably difficult to establish such an inward self-understanding for anyone living today, much less one who lived two thousand years ago.

Even in the case of a prolific writer about whom much biographical material is available, such as Augustine, Luther, or Teresa of Avila, it still remains problematic as to precisely what view each took of himself or herself. In the case of complex and subtle writers such as Kierkegaard and Thomas Wolfe, who spoke through parables, pseudonyms, and alter ego characters, it is much more difficult, even though an extensive corpus exists. The point: It is hardly fair to impose upon the historical study of Jesus requirements that would be considered outrageous demands if applied to other figures.

Suppose one is reading a brief biographical report of one's own life and finds important items missing. Would not the one who had lived the life know more about it than the biographer? Wouldn't one feel that some omissions would be tolerable because everything could not be said in a few pages? But wouldn't one also feel that some omissions are intolerable if they omit the heart of the matter! Christians believe that the canon contains the heart of the matter, sufficient for the salvation of humanity—not everything, but enough.

The "Hypothesized Document" Game

Is the proclamation of Christ detachable from the history of Jesus? Some influential traditions of modern inquiry into Jesus from Hegel and Strauss to Bultmann and Tillich have disavowed a major premise of classic Christianity: that the eventful history of Jesus is the undetachable basis for Christian teaching of Christ and salvation. Classic Christian teaching argues that there is a palpable continuity between the events of Jesus' ministry and the report of those events in the Gospels.

No one who reads the Epistles alongside the Synoptic Gospels can fail to sense enormous differences between them. In the Epistles little is said of the historical life of Jesus or the narratives of his ministry. In the Gospels we are constantly presented with an active, lively, historical figure who preaches, heals, teaches, prays, sweats, and interacts, while in the Epistles the focus is upon the interpretation of his ministry, particularly his death and resurrection.

Modern critical speculation has often concluded that there are in fact two very different Jesuses: the one actual and the other later proclaimed; one ignorant, the other projected as omniscient; one born of woman, the other supposedly born of a virgin. Accordingly, the historical Jesus is thought to be vastly unlike the Jesus Christ proclaimed by the remembering church.

Jesus is portrayed pseudocritically as an eschatological prophet who pointed toward the coming reign of God but not the Messiah who inaugurated it, as a teacher of high ethical perception but not God incarnate. The speculative critics conclude that Jesus did not view himself as Messiah or Son of God, but proclaimed the coming reign of God in such a forceful way that Paul and others were able later to attribute such terms to Jesus. But where did Paul get these ideas? Wrede thought they came from circles of hellenizing Judaism with which Jesus had no contact. Bultmann thought that a key piece of the puzzle was taken from a hypothesized gnostic redeemer myth and applied to Christ by Paul. In any case, the Jesus Christ who was remembered was thought to be radically different from Jesus himself. The extent of this difference is the major point in question.

If one takes the unlikely premise that Paul did not derive his view of Jesus Christ from Jesus Christ but from somewhere else, then one has an entirely new game to play historically: trying to find which streams from the history of religions might have been chosen to make up these interpretations. And if one cannot actually find documents, one may always hypothesize or fantasize them. Much so-called critical inquiry into Christian origins has had this speculative, fantasizing character, based on the shaky presupposition of radical disjunctiveness between Jesus and Paul.

A far more plausible hypothesis is that no one other than the Christ of the synoptics could have inaugurated the messianic reign of God that Paul saw as fulfilled in Jesus Christ. The classic assumption is that there is significant continuity between Jesus and Paul, the synoptics and the Epistles, the proclamation of the kingdom and the teaching of the Savior, and that the New Testament has a single basic Christology with numerous language variants. When these are separated artificially into rival Christologies or competing teachings, the steady unity of the New Testament is lost or misplaced.

The modern student of Scripture is sometimes left adrift with a curious irony: It appears that Jesus knew less about himself than did his interpreters, according to many critics, for he knew nothing of his own messiahship or divine sonship. On this basis it becomes difficult if not impossible to build a plausible Christology out of a naive, mistaken, hapless, or ignorant Jesus.

There is extraordinary hubris in this speculative pseudo-critical imagination, yet it must be said that it dominates much recent Scripture scholarship in the universities, even though it has hardly gained the slightest footing in the worshiping communities. The hubris lies in the assumption that only we in the twentieth century have finally found out about Jesus, about whom all previous centuries had wholly mistaken attitudes. Those who make much of the importance of this supposed discovery, however, number only a comparatively few influential scholars in academic centers whose reputations and grant-proposals often depend upon constantly new "finds" and monographs.

If so, why should Christian teaching trouble itself inordinately with this wayward and perverse academic arena? It must to some degree, because within the sphere of the university, these spokespersons may be heard as if they were speaking for the whole church about Jesus Christ. Christianity cannot disavow the universities it has created.

8

The Limits of
Historical Method

The Spirit continues to use historical inquiry as a refining fire to purge from religious faith unwarranted assumptions and needless cultural accretions, to intensify ethical awareness, and to enrich the memory of revelation. Historical inquiry, even when shaped by bias or outright rejection of Christianity, may still be used providentially as an instrument by which the Spirit curbs inordinate assertiveness, leads to faith, and judges sin.

Even scholarship which is hostile to religion can still provide data and hypotheses for examination which faith can use to turn human wrath to God-pleasing praise (Athenagoras, *A Plea For the Christians*, ANF, II, 129–48; Augustine, *The City of God*, I–IV, NPNF, 1 II, 1–84; Francis Hall, *Dogmatic Theology*, VI, 29). Gregory Nazianzen supplied a comic analogy: "As we have compounded healthful drugs from certain of the reptiles, so from secular literature we have received principles of enquiry and speculation, while we have rejected their idolatry" (Orat. XLIII.11, NPNF, 2 VII, 399).

If critical scholarship could be relieved of some of its unnecessary excesses, it could render a more lasting service of pruning and ethical deepening for Christian teaching. Yet modern critical scholarship is tryannized by postulates that make textual misinterpretations likely and predictable (M. Hengel, *Kerygma und Dogma*, 2 [1973], 85–90).

Jesus has been studied as an object of historical research by supposedly "scientific" methods. But there are severe limits to this approach. For history does not yield easily to the normal processes of verification expected in the hard sciences.

"The 'historical Jesus' is a technical phrase designating a hypothetical Jesus who could be interpreted exclusively in human, ordinary historical categories" (Ladd, *A Theology of the New Testament*, 178). As most commonly used, it indicates only "what can be known of Jesus of Nazareth by means of the scientific methods of the historian" (Robinson, *The New Quest for the Historical Jesus*, 26).

Historical study seeks to approach the past event through documentary, archaeological, and other types of evidence. The historian is not the lord of the evidence but the follower of it (Eusebius, *Church History*, VI.20–30, NPNF, 2 I, 268–76; Hippolytus, *The Refutation of All Heresies*, VII.17–26, ANF, V, 110-16; V. Harvey, *The Historian and the Believer* hereafter H&B, 54–59). Historical inquiry is hedged by hard limits (phenomena, documentation, verification):

(1) *The limits of what can be seen.* The phenomenal surface that can be grasped by evidence is far more fragile and vulnerable in the study of history than testable, repeatable experiments of physics, for history unlike physics cannot be repeated or objectively tested. Only phenomena are visible. As the soul (*psuche, anima*) of an organism cannot be seen or dissected, neither can the inner vitality of an event (Origen, Ag. Celsus, I.40–48, ANF, IV, 413–17).

When historians imitate hard scientists, the remembered events have an artificially molded character, having been molded to alien assumptions and predisposing questions. In science only the outer, observable surface (phenomena) can be measured and reported empirically. Some modern historians have been foolish in thinking it wise to search only for the hard evidences of the outer surfaces of events.

(2) *The limits of documentation.* All reported events depend upon documentation. All documentation, since written by human hands in human societies, is the expression of human passions and social interests that shape the report. They are "events" only because they are important to someone, and important to someone because one has an

interest in them (Dilthey, *Meaning in History*, 113–59); cf.
John 20:31; Calvin, *Commentaries*, XVIII, 281, 282; Harvey,
H&B). The hope for a totally disinterested reading of history
is a fantasy of interested readers who deceive themselves,
pretending to see history from some objective point outside of
history.

(3) *The limits of verification.* The heart of scientific
method is verification. Historians cannot achieve verification,
since the events have disappeared into the past. History
cannot be reenacted. There is something amusing about the
spectacle of historians seeking absolute verification. Proximate verification must depend upon the testimony of witnesses and the evidence of past documents fairly and
honestly analyzed. The documents of ancient history are
available largely on a chance (not a rational or equal or
deliberate or extensive) basis, whereas evidences of physics
are everywhere available for current experimentation. These
factors limit historical inquiry so as to make it nonanalogous
with physics and hard science. Humility is called for on every
hand in the study of history (Karl R. Popper, *The Poverty of
Historicism*).

When historians pretend to be behavioral scientists, they
necessarily distort the truth of history by admitting only
selected, preferred types of evidence, sometimes omitting
more illuminating evidence. This results in the odd situation
that historical study itself may elicit a loss and diminution of
historical truth, insofar as the scientific historian is only
willing to listen to what he already agrees with philosophically. Modern historical science thus both reveals and conceals
history—revealing what its philosophical assumptions admit
and concealing what its philosophical assumptions resist;
beholding the external phenomena and concealing the inner
truth. The study of Jesus has been too heavily indebted to
such assumptions (P. Althaus, *Fact and Faith in the Kerygma
of Today*, 60–74).

The irreducible characteristics of history affect all historical
study, and therefore the study of the history of Jesus. History
flows like time in linear, unrevisitable moments. Since
history recounts the exercise of human freedom, history is
intrinsically unpredictable.

After any event occurs, it is forever unalterable. Every now is unique—a special moment of opportunity that will be forever gone the next instant. Analogies may bridge these varied moments, but there are always more dissimilarities than similarities. Those who admit as historical only those events that correspond by analogy with familiar history (following Troeltsch on the law of analogy, *Theologie als Wissenschaft*, 108) persist in practicing a systematic distortion.

The course of history is no more certainly predictable scientifically than the course of a personal biography. For there are always possibilities of reversal of whatever trends prevail at any moment. Predictions based on the extrapolation of present trends are notoriously vulnerable because freedom can and usually does reverse established trends.

Which Events Are Admissible as "Historical"?

When the study of Jesus is limited to the scientific study of phenomena, what must be ruled out before the inquiry begins? The historical method used in modern biblical criticism searches for that which is demonstrable according to documentation that is acceptable to "modern consciousness," which itself is often defined by elites in cramped, wooden, reductionist terms. This is the loaded philosophical baggage that is assiduously carried wherever the biblical critic travels.

The actual historical event (historical truth as experienced and understood by human beings in real situations where decisions are actually being made) tends to elude such a constricted process of documentary verification, especially when the historian desires compulsively to control and channel the flow of evidence. The unwished result: Only those events that are tested and passed by reductionistic "historical critical methods" are judged authentic and presented as "historical" events.

The key test case for Christianity is the resurrection. If one begins by assuming that a resurrection cannot be an event in history, then one may confidently conclude that Jesus did not rise from the dead even before hearing the evidence. For one has decided in advance that whatever evidence is presented, it cannot be credited as an actual historical event. Pannenberg rightly argues that it is the task of Christology to base on the history of Jesus the true perception of his significance which is grasped only in relation to the resurrection (*Jesus: God and Man*, 29, 30). Such an effort requires a redefinition of historical evidence so as to include events frequently excluded by historians from the range of historical possibles.

The methodological approaches applied in the scientific laboratory are less appropriate to the study of history than are the less certain attempts to establish evidence through testimony in a court of law. The court attempts to establish the truth concerning persons and unrepeatable events. The scientific laboratory seeks to grasp the truth of objects, not persons, and of how causes can produce repeatable effects. In that sense the problems of establishing historical evidence are more like the problems of the court than of the laboratory.

History is even more evasive than the law, however, for unlike the courts, historical study does not permit active cross-examination of witnesses. Yet even when witnesses are intensely cross-examinable, the courtroom conflict situation may conceal as well as reveal the truth. In a similar way, the special ethos of critical inquiry may tend to conceal as well as reveal the truth about Jesus Christ. In either courtroom or history class the subtleties of actual past events always elude absolute verification.

Historical critics are fond of making pious statements about how history is sharply distinguished from faith. In doing so they intend to show that historical judgments are based upon objective fact, and that judgments shaped by faith are to be ruled out. Meanwhile it is not difficult to catch the critics red-handed offering as statements of fact views that actually amount to biased personal preferences (Maier, EHCM, 1–26; cf. Hippolytus, *Refut. of All Her.*, X, ANF, II, 140–53). These preferences often have a distinct aroma of social location, commonly dominated by the sociology of professionalization among guild scholars in biblical criticism whose future careers depend upon hewing the line. The New Testament documents do not deal with the fact of God in time as if apart from faith. Nor do they attest faith without recounting a straightforward history of the events of the theandric person, the God-man (Tertullian, *Against Marcion*, IV, 1–10, ANF,

III, 345–60; Athanasius, *Four Discourses Ag. Arians*, I.11–
21, NPNF, 2 IV, 312–19).

Deciding the Question before the Investigation

Often the procedure of historical biblical criticism has
required first the removal of all claims of revelation, and then
imposed upon all testimony the *a priori* claim that divine
disclosure is impossible. To assume before one begins the
investigation that revelation is irrelevant or impossible is to
decide in advance the most important question before making
the investigation.

Yet such is the procedure of much Scripture criticism,
which starts with a predisposing theory and philosophy
through which to filter selected facts, ruling out alleged facts
that do not fit into naturalistic assumptions. If one rules out
before one begins historical inquiry the premise that God can
come to save humanity, then one has systematically biased
the inquiry, whatever the rhetoric. William James stated the
procedural point well: "A rule of thinking which would
absolutely prevent me from acknowledging certain kinds of
truth, if those kinds of truth were really there, would be an
irrational rule" (W. James, *The Will to Believe*, 28).

This evasive procedure has comic qualities not unlike
those noticed by Gregory Nazianzen: "A man who states what
God is not without going on to say what He is acts much in
the same way as one would who when asked how many twice
five make, should answer, 'Not two, nor three, nor four, nor
twenty, nor thirty, nor in short any number below ten, nor any
multiple of ten;' but would not answer 'ten' " (Orat. XXVIII.9,
NPNF, 2 VII, 291).

The Risk One Takes in Studying Jesus

It may seem that criticism of the New Testament has
already "destroyed for good and all the possibility of touching
the real Jesus" (Mackintosh, *The Person of Jesus Christ*, 311).
But if the power of Jesus to transform life is able to be
undermined by historical inquiry, it cannot be the power of
God. Historical inquiry may pretend to have succeeded in

such an undermining, but whether it has is not for scholars to judge but history itself.

Meanwhile the historian remains a human being. No one is a historian alone without at the same time being a human being. Historical study does not proceed without conscience or adventure. Even historians may suddenly fall into the hands of the living God (Barth, *Romans; Church Dogmatics*, IV/2, 34ff.).

This is why skeptical historians who read the New Testament run the risk of being transformed by it (Kierkegaard, *Training in Christianity*, hereafter TC, 26–39). For the person of Jesus comes with the texts of the New Testament, communicating his own distinctive authority to any serious reader.

The Offense

The Incarnation was from the outset an offense (*skandalon*, Matt. 16:23; 18:7; Luke 17:1; Gal. 5:11) to its hearers. It remains an offense in modern society, and nowhere more so than in the self-assured sphere of the university. Christianity must clash with any fixed assumption that wishes inconspicuously to deprive Christianity of its central premise (Kierkegaard, *Two Ages:* TC, 79–132; cf. Eusebius, *The Proof of the Gospel*, I, 159).

It remains an important task of Christian teaching to state that offense clearly, let it happen, not try to prevent it, and in fact require it to be met and examined. The offense is much more resilient than first-century cosmology, which demythologizers confused with the offense. The offense is Christ himself.

Can moderns understand the salvation of which Scripture speaks? The supposed gulf between modern and premodern consciousness may not be as vast as imagined by the prototypical accommodators to modernity (Schleiermacher, Hegel, Strauss, Biedermann, Brightman, Bultmann, and Tillich). Many persons with views thought to be premodern still seem to be very much around in scientific circles long after they were expected (by Feuerbach, Nietzsche, Freud, Bertrand Russell, Bonhoeffer, and Gogarten) to have atrophied and disappeared.

We have been told that modern ears simply cannot hear classic Christian language, cannot bear to hear of sin, incarnation, atonement, sacrifice, resurrection, or salvation. This highly questionable premise has spurred Christianity's premature accommodation to a demoralized modernity.

It is demeaning to modern consciousness to say that it is incapable of understanding something that has been understood in premodern periods. This is comparable to the demeaning view that young persons are incapable of sexual fidelity or continence, as if to say: Human beings cannot do that anymore. That can easily become a dishonoring of human freedom.

According to this interpretation, Christianity must repackage the gospel into categories that modernity finds palatable and understandable. So we borrow Marxist language and talk of class analysis, or we borrow process categories and talk of the distinction between the primordial and consequent nature of God (itself unknowingly borrowed from classical Christianity), or we appropriate Freudian categories and talk of projection and sublimation. What "modern man" (mostly our overgeneralized fantasy) will or will not find acceptable (according to some elitist assessment) has become the prevailing tryanny of modern "critical" Scripture study.

Despite all predictions, vital forms of orthodoxy appear to be steadily strengthening and increasing in the postmodern period. Not only in Christianity and Judaism but in Islamic and Buddhist cultures do we find a resilient postmodern capacity for traditional religion. The renewal of orthodoxy within postliberal Judaism is a profound case in point. The vitality of the pan-Orthodox movement of various Eastern Christian traditions is an even more remarkable signal. The embryonic signs of emergence of a postmodern orthodoxy among liberal and evangelical Protestants are abounding and promising.

Experimental "Christ"-ologies

Let us suppose that the Gospels are interpretations of the remembering church projected back upon imagined "events" of Jesus' unknowable life. By this device there is provided the appearance of having intellectually discredited virtually all of the primary themes of classic Christian teaching: pre-existence of the eternal Logos, the sonship of Christ, his sinlessness, and his atoning death, resurrection, and ascension. According to such modern "Christ"-ological speculation, the memory of Jesus Christ is largely a history of mistakes.

There is a strong smell of hubris that accompanies this sort of critical pretense. It seems to be historically sophisticated while putting a spin on the historical evidence so as to make it align with presuppositions acceptable within certain circles of modern consciousness. It assumes that modern consciousness is self-evidently wiser and superior to all premodern ideas and conceptions and value-commitments (Nietzsche, "Why I am So Clever," *Ecce Homo*, 236–58; cf. Jacques Derrida, *Archeology of the Frivolous*). Fortunately, the black church and Third World Christianity have not become trapped in such an elitism.

In such modern "soter"-iologies an extremely anti-Protestant premise takes hold: that only professional or technical experts can rightly read Holy Writ. Radical criticism has become the Protestant intellectual equivalent of papal infallibility. The new pope is a professor; the new *curia* a professional society for Scripture critics. This elicits a professional elitism contrary to the Protestant spirit of lay reading of Scripture. It is a *magisterium* far more restrictive than any known in medieval scholasticism. Classic ecumenical Christianity has become misplaced amid these speculations. The procedure keeps the names and retains some of the forms of religion but lacks the power of godly religion, yet it proceeds with a defensive or sentimental (or economic!) attachment to the institutions that have followed from Christ's life and work (Kierkegaard, *Judge for Yourselves!*). Such has occurred in the period of Christological reasoning from Hegel to Tillich, the period of accelerating modern experimentation in "Christ"-ologies.

Luther could not understand why those who hate the Bible cannot seem to leave it alone: "Whoever has not accepted or will not accept perfectly and purely this Man, called Jesus Christ, God's Son, whom we Christians are preaching, should let the Bible rest in peace. This is my advice. He will certainly take offense and become blinder and madder the longer he studies" (Luther, Sermon on 2 Sam. 23:1–7, 1543, *What Luther Says*, I, 148, Weimar, 54, 29).

James Barr, a leading biblical critic, blatantly states the reductionist premise: "My account of the formation of the biblical tradition is an account of a *human* work. It is *man's* statement of his beliefs, the events he has experienced, the stories he has been told, and so on" (Barr, *The Bible in the Modern World*, 120). Origen expressed the mind of the believing church that the Holy Scriptures are not finally reducible to "human compositions," but written by historical persons "by inspiration of the Holy Spirit," so as to become "transmitted and entrusted to us by the will of God" (*De Princip.*, IV.I.9, ANF, IV, 357).

What to Do with Modernity as a Decision for Christology

Modern Christian leaders of all sorts are worried about the loss of vitality in the church—most dramatically in liberal Protestantism with its precipitous loss of church members, and in liberal Roman Catholicism with its crisis of authority and demise of priestly vocations.

Two hypotheses compete head on. Some believe that Christianity has not accommodated itself sufficiently to modernity. Others argue that Christianity has accommodated itself too cheaply to modernity during the time in which modernity is rapidly deteriorating. The latter hypothesis seems much closer to the evidence (S. Findeisen, H. Frey, W. Johanning, *Das Kreuz Jesu und die Krise der Evangelischen Kirche*; G. Bergmann and H. Diem, *Das gleiche Evangelium*).

Whichever path one might take, it seems evident that Christology has a powerful impact for good or ill upon church praxis. Where ancient ecumenical teaching of Jesus Christ is neglected, sermons resort to truisms and moralisms, ethical vitality is vitiated, and religious institutions become quickly demoralized. Where Christ is misplaced, humanitarian acts may remain, medical and relief work may continue, and political action may work for humane interests, yet these often lack the spiritual and moral vitality of that life which is hid in Christ. The deteriorations of modern church life have their main cause in the abandonment of classic Christology.

Christology today must be attempted amid the collapse of modernity. We live in the midst of that collapse. We have no other choice than a postmodern Christology.

The Life of Jesus Is That of the Incarnate Lord

Jesus' life cannot be recounted as if it were only a supertemporal divine event. For it is the story of a human being. Nor can it be told as if it were merely the story of an ordinary individual. For in this individual we behold God's own coming. His life story is a thoroughly human story, but at the same time it is the story of God's own coming. The account cannot be narrated without the theandric premise— truly God, truly human in one person.

We make sense of this history by making full use of historical method and testimony. But this does not imply that we cull out each and every reference to the divine initiative so as to rewrite the narrative and destroy the central datum to be investigated. The New Testament writers remembered better than they understood (V. Taylor, *The Person of Christ*; T. W. Manson, *Studies in the Gospels and Epistles*). They remembered with sufficient adequacy—sufficient for human salvation.

The burden of Christology is to show or disprove the premise that Jesus is the Christ, the incarnate Lord. The Christological arena has not yet been entered if that task is systematically evaded. If Jesus Christ is indeed Lord, then an inquiry into him that failed to notice that fact would be like an inquiry into jazz that never heard of New Orleans.

The truth of his life—that he was God incarnate—was not fully realized by most of his companions during his earthly life. It was only adequately grasped after his resurrection. Once understood, it became the central feature of apostolic teaching.

His life was the incomparable life of the God-man. If one gives up this premise in the interest of getting along with certain historians, one has thereby given up the key that makes the narratives of the New Testament make sense. For without this key, no passage of the New Testament yields to plausible analysis. Every text remains baffling without it.

The Word became flesh in a person in history. The uncreated One assumed the life of a creature. God entered history and became a single individual in it. Let this theandric premise be taken seriously and the study of the historical Jesus can once again be resumed.

9

Resurrection:
Christ's and Ours

In order to grasp what the resurrection meant to the followers of Jesus, it is necessary to ask what the prevailing idea of general resurrection meant among Jews in the period preceding Jesus. Everyone in that context knew exactly what resurrection meant: the anticipated end of history. The general resurrection was precisely the event that was expected to happen at the end of time. The dead would rise and be judged. It was in that frame of reference that a powerful hope intensified in the century prior to Jesus that the end time would occur soon and the will of God would be finally revealed. End-time communities such as those on the Dead Sea were rigorously readying themselves for the consummation of history, for the resurrection of the just and the unjust.

The underlying assumption was that the meaning of history would be fully known only at its end. If God makes himself known in history, then it is evident that we do not know the whole story until the end. So we do not learn the will of God merely by looking at a phase or part of the historical process anymore than we understand a novel only by reading until the middle chapter. We grasp the full meaning only by reading the whole, as concluded by its last page.

Similarly, the meaning of one's own personal history is not fully revealed as long as one is still living. Something decisive might happen at some future date that would change substantially the meaning of one's present existence. So it seemed to Jewish prophetic consciousness that the meaning of history could finally be revealed only at its end. And what was to happen at the end? Resurrection. The dead would rise for final judgment.

The Event Named "Resurrection"

Whatever it was that occurred after Jesus' crucifixion, one thing is absolutely clear: It was *called* "resurrection." Of that there can be no doubt. All who were met by it called it the same thing. However unclear many things may be about alleged meetings with Jesus after his death, there was a consensus in the community that whatever it was that people were experiencing, the correct term for it was *resurrection*. This meant that they had experienced and tasted the first fruits of the expected event at the end time of judgment and redemption.

Suppose general resurrection were Event Z. Suppose there was a widely held consensus prior to Jesus about what Event Z would look like and what would happen then. Jesus came, lived, and died. After his death a series of occurrences took place that were clearly called and by many consensually identified as Z.

The significance of this is awesome: The events surrounding Jesus' death were experienced as the fulfillment of history, the decisive event of the last days, or the decisive anticipation of the final event of history that reveals God's will once for all. So even though history continued to occur after Jesus died and rose again, there was a sense in which Christians understood themselves through their meeting with Jesus to be in touch with the end time, and therefore with the meaning of universal history!

This empowered the early Christian community with incredible courage in the face of seemingly impossible obstacles and terrifying threats. Why? Because their trust was not in this broken world but in the risen Christ present to them as they sat together "at the Lord's Table" or faced the wild animals of the Roman Colosseum.

Suppose the prophets were right, that God's will is revealed through historical events, and hence that God's will is *finally* knowable only at the conclusion of the drama of history. Theology would then be intent on trying to understand, if possible, the anticipated *end* of the process, beyond all current historical alienations, finitude, blindness, and sin.

The earliest church reasoned in this way: In Jesus' resurrection the end is already present, in an anticipated sense. Thus the will of God is finally revealed. So to participate in Christ is already to share in the events of the last days. It all made reasonable sense, seen from within the assumptions of Jewish historical reasoning, transformed by a living encounter with the resurrected Jesus.

We today must learn to think historically in the Hebraic sense if we are to make sense of this central proclamation of Christianity. Seen in this frame of reference, the resurrection is so decisive that the importance of all other theological issues pales beside it. It focuses on nothing less than the final revelation of the will of God in history.

We are searching for the center of the wide circumference of Christian experience. What is the center? *Resurrection* as interpersonal meeting with the living Christ. Not resurrection as idea or past event but resurrection as a currently experienced interpersonal encounter. This is why interpersonal meeting has been the central feature of Christian theology from its inception.

Something so decisive happened anticipatively for human history in the resurrection of Jesus that it does not and cannot fit into our ordinary categories of understanding. We cannot rule out the resurrection of Jesus simply on the grounds (as Troeltsch's law of analogy would require) that nothing like this ever happened to us before. How could it! The event of which Christianity speaks is, like all truly significant interpersonal meeting, an event without analogy.

The least plausible of all explanations of the resurrection was that it was generated out of the despairing imagination of the disciples. For that does not explain why they were willing to risk their lives for it. Nor does it account for one of the most characteristic literary features of the Easter narratives: the report that the beholders were utterly surprised by the appearance of the risen Lord. The "surprise" element of the Easter narratives is too recurrent to be considered an anomaly. It is not likely that one would report being surprised by something that one had previously projected. No. *Something* occurred in Jesus' resurrection. It is quite unconvincing to assume that it could have been nothing. Whatever it was, it was experienced as the resurrected or spiritual or glorified body of Jesus and understood as the final self-disclosure of God.

Classical Christianity is saturated with this language about resurrection—both Christ's and ours. When the apostles began to try to express what had happened to them, they did not begin with a system of metaphysics or ethical injunctions or scientific data. Rather, they began with experiential testimony of an interpersonal meeting with the risen Christ that "made all things new." All other forms of knowing were seen in relation to their being known in this way by God.

Once that point is grasped, everything else in Christianity falls into place. Human encounter is seen in relation to the divine human encounter. Our walk through daily life is understood as *participatio Christi*. Pastoral care becomes an active sharing in the life of Christ. Preaching is the announcement of the coming of the risen Christ into ordinary human life. The Eucharist is the presence of Christ experienced sacramentally as end-time banquet. The moral life is grasped essentially as the sharing of the love of God in and for the world.

If so, then the central event upon which Christian teaching rests has always been Cross-and-Resurrection. It remains the perennial agenda for theology.

Admittedly, the term "liberation theology" has suffered from overexpectation and the rhetoric of messianic idealism, but there is at least one sense in which Christian believers of all ages have understood themselves as being liberated: freed by the risen Christ from the power of sin and death, liberated *for* the neighbor and *from* self-justifying defensiveness, liberated *by* God *to* the life of responsible freedom in the world. "If then the Son sets you free, you will indeed be free" (John 8:36). "You see, then, my brothers, we are no slave-woman's children; our mother is the free woman. Christ set us free, to be free men. Stand firm, then, and refuse to be tied to the yoke of slavery again" (Gal. 4:31–5:1). "The life-giving law of the Spirit has set you free from the law of sin and death" (Rom. 8:2). "Live as free men, yet without using your

freedom as a pretext for evil; but live as servants of God"
(1 Peter 2:16 RSV).

Shall We Sin That Grace May Abound?

But—now we hesitate. If Christ forgives sin, isn't there an
ethical embarrassment at the heart of Christianity? Does not
unmerited grace invite gross irresponsibility? Does it not
tempt us merely to follow our self-assertive interests and then
point cheaply to God's patient, unconditional, ever-available
forgiveness?

Is not Christianity of this sort potentially the least moral of
all religions, precisely *because* of forgiveness? The same
basic query was thrown at Paul: "Are we to continue in sin
that grace may abound?" (Rom. 6:1 RSV). Paul's answer hinges
on this penetrating analogy: You are dead in Christ—dead to
the old, alive to the new; dead to sin, alive to grace. Why
should you foolishly continue to live as if you were dead?

In seeking to answer this objection responsibly, classical
Christianity has always had to stress not only that God in
Christ offers pardon for our sins but also that he provides a
community of birth and nurture, a context for actualizing
freedom from bondage to sin, a *koinonia* in which love can be
felt and experienced. To the preaching of the pardoning
verdict of justification (what God does *for* us to right our
fallen existence) must be added a concern for daily feeding in
a family and an order of governance by which the believer is
drawn increasingly into the life of faith, hope, and love. In
traditional terms, this work of grace is called sanctification,
which concerns what God does *in* us to bring us to the
fulfillment of our human possibility, by grace working with
our wills. The bare word of unconditional pardon would be
scandalously immoral without a community concerned with
the ever-deepening growth of persons toward maturity in
Christ and deeper participation in God's mission of love for
the world. Christianity hopes that both persons and social
processes will in some measure be redeemed from sin in fact
and not merely in principle.

Suppose a governor decides to render a formal pardon for a
criminal. He signs the paper, and the act goes into effect. But

that does not necessarily mean that the criminal will be remotivated toward responsible behavior. The pardon is not in itself a behavioral guarantee.

Similarly, classical Christianity has concerned itself not merely with toothless talk of God's pardon, but more so with a supportive community and a structure for moral development by which that pardon might become appropriated in the life of responsible love. This requires a nurturing environment, a Eucharistic community, a context in which the pardoned person can come increasingly to live in Christ, not in name only but in deed and truth. This growing process itself is the work of God the Spirit, encouraging and inspiring our own spirits freely to respond. The same God who meets us in the pardoning event of the living Christ is at work in this community, its preaching, sacraments, and discipline.

There is an ongoing debate among Christians whether this process of growth is ever fully completed or in principle even actualizable so long as we remain "in the flesh"—entangled in the history of sin. Most Lutheran and Reformed teachers have generally doubted that perfect love is possible in this life, while Catholic, Greek Orthodox, Anglican, and Methodist traditions have tended to say that we cannot put arbitrary limits on the ability of God the Spirit to refashion our lives.

In all these traditions, however, there is an underlying consensus that grace seeks to enable a life of radical responsiveness to the love of God. If we have received the love of God, we are called to love as we have been loved, forgive as we have been forgiven, be merciful to others even as God is merciful to us.

If good works never flow as a fruit of faith, there remains some doubt about the genuineness of faith. Not that we are saved by these good works—never. We are saved by grace alone. But we are being called to respond to that active grace with active good works, sharing the self-giving love of God in Christ with the neighbor. In this way, the body of Christ becomes manifested through our bodies. This mystery is beautifully stated in Ephesians 2:10 RSV:"For we are [God's own] workmanship, created in Christ Jesus for good works."

10

The Expurgated
Scripture

I recognized in myself some time ago a fixed habit that many share. In a casual, straight read-through of the New Testament, I suddenly became aware that I had been consistently neglecting a certain portion of the New Testament, seldom preaching on it, and never including it as a deliberate focus for my personal theological reflection and teaching. I speak of the Pastoral Epistles (1 and 2 Timothy and Titus) and the General, or Catholic, Epistles (James, 1 and 2 Peter, the letters of John, and Jude).

When I tried to understand why these later writings had been given low priority in my thinking, it required a rehearsal of the major influences on my reading of the New Testament: Rudolf Bultmann, Ernst Käsemann, Günther Bornkamm, and others, all highly respected leaders in New Testament interpretation. What follows is an attempt to track down the reasons why this pivotal part of Scripture has seemed relatively closed to modern consciousness and to suggest how it might be reopened.

This chapter asks: Can the Pastoral and General Epistles of the New Testament help us reset the agenda for theology? I will show how and why these letters have been discounted by leading biblical scholars. And I will ask whether these writings nonetheless provide a rich mine of insights directly relevant to the situation of Christian ministry within modernity. I intend to address the working pastor more than the professional exegete, but the line of argument also impinges on the way one might proceed to teach New Testament either in a church or university setting.

Systematic Neglect of the Pastoral and General Epistles

Two scholars in particular, Rudolf Bultmann and Ernst Käsemann, have shaped a skeptical attitude toward the later New Testament writings. Both are highly influential—so much so that it would be hard to cite any New Testament interpreters more widely respected since Albert Schweitzer. I am not suggesting that they generally agree, for Käsemann has frontally challenged the Bultmannians on many assumptions, but they do agree firmly on the main point at issue in this chapter: that the Pastoral and General Epistles on the whole represent a regrettable deterioration of the normative (Pauline) theology of the New Testament. I would prefer, however, to let them speak for themselves in establishing this point.

For years I have approached Bultmann with sympathy and appreciation, for he more than anyone in the 1950s helped the New Testament come alive for me. On the point at issue in this chapter, I feel that I must have unconsciously colluded with him, along with many others, in chipping away at the New Testament canon in a way that has resulted in significant theological and pastoral losses.

Bultmann's account of the later writings runs like this. By the time of the Pastoral Epistles, faith (*pistis*) had become little more than a defensive piety trying to make "a place for itself within the framework of bourgeois living" (*Theology of the New Testament*, hereafter TNT, 1, 183). He describes the Pastorals as a "faded Paulinism" in which faith had become reduced to the "worn-down meaning of 'Christianity,' 'Christian religion,'" which signified little more than "right doctrine" or "orthodoxy" (TNT, 2, 183). The letter of James is even more depressing to Bultmann, since it lacks "every shred of understanding" of the eschatological hope that had energized the other (earlier, presumably normative) New Testament theologies. Bultmann regretted that in James "the moralism of the synagogue-tradition had made its entry." He thought it is possible that its author even "took over a Jewish document and only lightly retouched it." Bultmann testily argued that 2 Peter, like James, never got beyond "legalistic moralism." He regarded it as a major theological setback that Christ was seen as a "pattern" for the believer. Similarly, Jude was thought to be moralistic and overly concerned with "pure living" ethics (TNT, 2, 163–69). In these later writings, according to Bultmann, "sinlessness had thereby become a task to be accomplished." "In no case is conversion understood as the radical transformation of the old man," and salvation is "reduced to an event—the death and resurrection of Jesus—the effect of which, when appropriated in baptism, is to cancel the sins of the past" (TNT, 2, 204–09). Bultmann bemoans as sad evidence of theological deterioration (!) the fact that in the Pastorals "the demand for good works is everywhere heard" (TNT, 2, 211).

Käsemann extended this polemic by disparaging the Pastoral Epistles as a "case study in narrow-mindedness." In his view, "the gospel is domesticated," "early Christian prophecy is greatly restricted," and the church is trapped in a mood of "introversion," seeking to achieve a "halo of legitimacy" (*Jesus Means Freedom*, hereafter JMF, 88–97). According to Käsemann, the Pastorals have stupidly misunderstood Paul's theology, have "levelled it out," while freedom has become a private affair, stuffily "churchified," and the focus shifted to "the apostolic succession of the episcopal office," which, quips Käsemann, is "one of the many Christian fictions" (JMF, 97).

The General Epistles worry Käsemann even more. James' talk about "the perfect law, the law of liberty" (James 1:25 RSV) is viewed as nothing more than "pretty phrases," "ornaments" which smack of "slightly retouched Jewish traditions" (JMF, 86). Even worse, 2 Peter represents a "relapse of Christianity into hellenistic dualism"; "its eschatology lacks any vestige of Christological orientation" (*Essays on New Testament Themes*, hereafter Essays, 178–80). Phrases such as "Our Lord and Saviour" are viewed as impersonal "stereotypes" without spiritual power. In the post-Pauline writings, Jesus' "red-hot message" has been reduced "to room temperature," characterized by "admonitions to live a godly life in quietness and integrity" while "combined intolerably with the political maxim that calmness is the citizen's first duty" (JMF, 87).

By the time the Pastoral and General Epistles were written, "Pauline theology was forgotten and replaced" (Essays, 93). The blame for this deterioration is laid by Käsemann upon the growing influence, emanating from Jerusalem, of the Jewish Christian leaders who tamed down the Pauline view of charisma and woodenly replaced it with the traditional Jewish notion of ordination, which had "the same meaning as it has in Judaism: it is the bestowal of the Spirit and it empowers those who receive it to administer the *depositum fidei*" (Essays, 87). Käsemann concludes that Paul is later portrayed in Acts as if he were setting up presbyteries and trying to legitimate church order and apostolic succession as the guarantor of tradition, and Peter is later shown as if he were bestowing the apostolic blessing, inspecting churches, commissioning pastors, and participating in the laying on of hands. All of this Käsemann thinks was based upon a "fabricated chain of tradition" which "cannot possibly be harmonized" with Paul's theology, and even stands "in the starkest contradiction to it" (Essays, 87–92). He concludes his influential essay on "Paul and Nascent Catholicism" with this dismal irony: "The connection between Paul and the later period rested largely on misunderstanding" (Essays, 26).

This direction set by Bultmann and Käsemann (which can be detected earlier in the works of Rudolf Sohm and Martin Dibelius) is subsequently echoed by numerous contemporary New Testament scholars, from among whom I choose as a representative voice one who is often considered a moderate, mediating figure, Günther Bornkamm. Although Bornkamm makes the disclaimer that we would "do well not to censure the later writings in the New Testament canon by the theological standards of the previous age, or even of a later one," he nonetheless proceeds to do just that. Second Peter, he says, is "distinctly inferior to Paul's eschatology." "It is no longer the expression of a living faith. Not even the few impressive phrases it contains are enough to deceive the reader" (*The New Testament: A Guide to Its Writings*, hereafter NTGW, 127). The letter of James he considers hardly an improvement, for in it "faith is relegated so far into the background that we are tempted to ask if this letter was originally a Christian writing at all" (NTGW, 120). In the Pastoral Epistles he sees reflected only "a bourgeois ideal of Christian morality" (NTGW, 115).

This depressing majority position was much earlier expressed by Rudolf Sohm's radical view that any ecclesiastical rule or law is contradictory to the very nature of the believing community. Bultmann fatefully agreed with Sohm's antinomian-charismatic conception of the church "as a society constituted not by a code of law but by the sway of the Spirit. [Sohm] is right, further in maintaining that the congregation, so understanding itself, needs no law; in fact that legal regulation contradicts the Church's nature" (TNT, II, 97ff.). One might dismiss such a view as the petty, partisan polemics of Protestant individualism were it not for the fact that this view has been widely adopted by influential New Testament scholars, with the post-Bultmannians still exercising a wide influence among New Testament scholars in Europe and America.

When I began to ask how I had adopted the attitude that these later letters are of minimal theological importance, it dawned on me how deeply I, along with many others, have been affected by a strong tradition of highly esteemed New Testament scholarship, very existentialist in its psychological predispositions, that has, in the name of objective historical scholarship, carried on a constant polemic against the tradition-nurturing and proto-catholic impulses of the New Testament—against its struggle with heresy, its attempt to develop an ordained succession of ministry, and its primitive attempts at church order.

The Fifth Gospel

This is no place to lay out a dreary string of supportive quotations to establish this point, but it would be easily conceded by most knowledgeable New Testament scholars— the prevailing opinion is that the Pastoral and General Epistles represent a depressing deterioration of earlier, vibrant New Testament theology and are far less important to us than Paul or the fourth gospel or the synoptics. Our task is to assess this consensus and its long-range consequences for our contemporary ailments in theology and ministry.

Under the tutelage of this critical school, chronological priority came to mean theological priority, and its inverse to imply inevitable deterioration. The canon within the canon became subtly redefined by historical-critical scholars, first by establishing a late chronology for these writings, then by declaring unfavorably on their pseudonymity, and finally by casting them into a kind of decanonized limbo by pronouncing their theology patently inferior.

Those familiar with the history of Protestantism, but less so with the recent history of the critical study of Scripture, might imagine that Protestant scholars would be vigorously defending canonical Scripture (following the Reformation principle of *sola scriptura*) and taking for granted the authority of the canon universally affirmed by classical Protestant and Catholic traditions. A closer inspection reveals that these scholars are prone to think quite idiosyncratically about a "canon within the canon," a fifth gospel (the slender one of the form critics) which becomes the normative standard for the other four. When the dust has settled, the operating assumption is usually that doctrinal (especially ecclesiological) questions are to be decided essentially on the grounds either of chronological priority or by means of comparison with normative Paulinism.

In this way canonicity itself has subtly become purely a matter of current (often faddish) historical-critical judgment! Käsemann, whose language tends to be more volatile than the others, resorts to the image of "freeing God" from the "imprisonment" of the canon (Essays, 105). For Käsemann, the function of the New Testament canon is less to constitute the foundation of the unity of the church than merely to "provide the basis for the multiplicity" of its confessions, which he believes to be enmeshed in "irreconcilable theological contradictions" (Essays, 100). Such statements, which would have been rejected out of hand by classical Protestant theologians, have of late taken on the solemn air of moral authority in some quarters of the community of biblical academics, which not surprisingly is in danger of becoming ever more estranged from the living mainstream of the worshiping Christian communities they once sought to serve.

Our steady hope in all this has been that the historians would make unprejudiced judgments about chronological priority and documentary authenticity, unaffected by hidden preconceptions. We have watched them assign their priorities, first to Paul, then to the synoptics and grudgingly to John, and last (and clearly least) to these later writings, often demeaned by terms such as "pseudo-Pauline" or "subapostolic" or "later pseudonymous writings." The hidden switch in this is that this order of priority directly corresponds with a silent predisposition to the tendency out of which all of these writers come: namely, the familiar polemic of the early Luther against medieval Catholicism, which becomes unconsciously reread back into the New Testament.

These historical critics thus solemnly rehearse the jaded Protestant myth that the earliest Christian communities had the purest doctrine, and that soon afterward the church "fell" into "organizational rigidities" and "catholic distortions." So part of the task of contemporary biblical scholarship is to battle the historical self-deceptions of New Testament exegetes who, under the guise of emptying themselves of prejudices, have reintroduced into biblical interpretation one of the most familiar of all Protestant prejudices. Under the presumption of historical objectivity they have restated the sixteenth-century triumphalist rhetoric against the catholicizing tendency.

In correcting this trajectory, we must not oppose historical-critical scholarship as such but rather look for a chastened, less self-deceptive form of it. Historical criticism must continue to do its work, but what it can never do is act as an authority for canonization. Historians do not have the authority for canonization. Historians do not have the authority to judge what is and is not canonical Scripture. Only the church, in ecumenical consensus, can make that judgment, as it did in its early period of formation.

Largely unnoticed in this polemic is the fact that this most recent pattern of canonical revisionism is hardly a new challenge for the Christian tradition. These efforts are strikingly similar to those of Marcion, the second-century heretic who proposed an abridged canon dominated by Paul, or portions of Paul, and sharply rejected the Pastoral and General Letters, admitted only a recension of the gospel of

Luke, and rejected the other three Evangelists. In his determined attempt to rid the church of what he regarded as un-Pauline ideas and remnants of Jewish influence, however, Marcion indirectly influenced the early church to respond by distinguishing between authentic and spurious documents, and in this sense became a major (though indirect) factor in the development of the traditional canon, which, of course, steadfastly embraced the Pastoral and General Epistles.

When we allow ourselves to be addressed by these letters, however, we discover to our amazement that they represent not a deterioration but a marvelously spirited, vital, and maturing phase of early Christian theological development. They struggle with the meaning of ordination, the continuity and stability of the tradition, the nature of the pastoral office, the criteria for doctrinal definition, and the distinction between heterodoxy and orthodoxy—all issues that face us today. These are problems that could not have been taken up until the church had gained several decades of experience and had faced up to the reality that it would have to continue to deal with ongoing history, governmental authority, and serious challenges to it from within and from without.

The Reversal of Decanonization

What benefits are we likely to experience by seeking to rescue the Pastoral and General Epistles from this strange status of unofficial decanonization? In what surprising ways are the contexts in which these letters were written similar to our own cultural dilemmas? These vital questions cannot be answered in a few neat sentences. They must remain on the agenda of theology until they are clearly worked through. But I will attempt at least an initial, minimal answer, which I hope might be improved with continued debate.

We will benefit by the study of the Pastoral and General Epistles today because they represent a maturing, not a degenerating, phase of early Christian theological development. The crucial question before the churches then was: How, in a period of cross-cultural pluralism, syncretism, political alienation, and vast historical mutation, is it possible to pass the tradition learned from the earliest Christians on to succeeding generations? How can we teach it accurately without distortions, and how can we defend it against interpretations that would profoundly diminish it? It is a life-and-death question that echoes in our situation today: Can the tradition be transgenerationally communicated amid a period of widespread social disruption?

It reveals a tedious lack of imagination to conclude that these writers' interest in historical continuity, unity, and tradition (which they solved successfully by means of ordination, the clear definition of apostolic teaching, a fierce struggle against heresy, and a stable church order) represented a disastrous setback in theology. If they had not done their job well in the period of the Pastoral and General Epistles, we would not be reading the rest of the New Testament now.

I do not imply that Paul or the Evangelists deserve any less study, but only that these pastoral writings deserve relatively more, partly to correct their long neglect, and partly because they speak so poignantly to our current pastoral struggles with anomie, social upheaval, antinomianism, and gnosticism.

PART THREE:

THE LIBERATION OF ORTHODOXY

The Christian intellect has no reason to be intimidated in the presence of later-stage deteriorating modernity. Christianity has seen too many supposedly modern eras to be cowed by this one. There is a quality of lightness that pervades classical Christianity's dialogue with modernity.

Christian freedom delights precisely in this world as the arena of God's providence. This age is the only one we have. There is no time for maudlin nostalgia. But the cloak of modernity should be worn lightly. It is not a tourniquet. There is no injunction against chuckling inwardly at the comic incongruities of modernity, and no need to lay on it a heavy blame trip.

Christian freedom is a quiet laughter, not the harsh laughter of a defensive apocalypticism that cannot distinguish a minor cultural crisis from the End of Days. It is a laughter rooted in unmerited grace and historical awareness that knows that it need not grovel before either the dogmas or the myopias of a particular time.

This freedom is what I prefer to call "liberated orthodoxy"—being freed, by historical perspective and evangelical faith, from the illusions of modernity and for Eucharistic existence. The campaign slogan might be: "Freedom now for tradition!" For Christianity has a right to be understood historically, as it has understood itself, even as every individual person has a right to be judged not merely in terms of present momentary transgressions but in terms of a larger lifelong intentionality and long-standing behavior patterns.

11

The Craft of Pastoral Guardianship

The sociology of orthodoxy is such an intriguing subject that it amazes me that it has been so avidly avoided by sociologists. Jewish, Islamic, and Christian sociologists whose temperament or value-commitments already lean toward tradition-maintenance have an exciting field of investigation awaiting them. It remains virgin territory intellectually, due to the preoccupation of sociological research with social *change* and the corollary bias against social continuity. In this respect, sociologists might do well to begin by studying the maintenance of tradition within their own sociology profession and the degree to which an official sociological doctrine or the apparatus of sociological orthodoxy already exists within their own journals and societies.

The premise of the sociology of any orthodoxy (Islamic, Skinnerian, Marxian, psychoanalytic, Jewish, Protestant, and so on) is this: If social processes are to achieve multigenerational continuity, they require legitimization and careful tradition-maintenance. Without any authorized definition of a movement's teaching, it cannot span the generations or even assess the validity of potential misinterpretations.

A religious tradition dissipates rapidly if it cannot distinguish itself in relation to its cultural alternatives. The attempt to provide clear and authoritative doctrinal definition in order to sustain the cohesive basis of the community is called orthodoxy. Although this process has been poorly understood sociologically, it exists in every human community that has intergenerational aspirations and certainly in all the great religious traditions.

The Sociology of Orthodoxy:
How Is It Illumined by the Jewish Experience?

Where did we get the twisted notion that orthodoxy is essentially a set of ideas rather than a living tradition of social experience? Our stereotype of orthodoxy is that of frozen dogma, rather than a warm continuity of human experience— of grandmothers teaching granddaughters, of feasts and stories, of rites and dancing. Orthodoxies are never best judged merely by their doctrinal ideas, but more so by their social products, the quality of their communities, their ability to nurture a tradition through multigenerational challenges, the variable ways they have found to sing, celebrate, marry, and bury. They await being studied sociologically, not just theologically.

Yet, in conversation with sociologists, I repeatedly asked them if they could think of a single definitive work on the sociology of orthodoxy, and they could not come up with any significant titles. I later made a bibliographical search myself to see if they were right, and to my amazement they were. There is a fair amount of talk about pattern-maintenance, legitimization, authority, and social control, but virtually none strictly speaking on orthodoxy as a sociological type.

Suppose a librarian decided to put all sociology books on rapid social change on a certain shelf and all those on the sociology of orthodoxy on the next shelf. Upon gathering the books she found that those studying rapid social change covered fifty shelves. Those on orthodoxy needed only a part of one shelf, and they were all so old they were falling to pieces. What would that tell you about the kinds of value judgments scholars have been making? I do not imply that rapid social change has been excessively studied, but that the dynamics of orthodoxy and tradition-maintenance have been neglected out of unconscious predispositions.

A New York museum presented an exhibit entitled "The Orthodox Experience," a powerful visual statement of the living social experience of Jewish orthodoxy. The focus properly was on the human experience, rather than merely on a set of abstract ideas. The exceptional delight expressed in this exhibit made me wonder why we have so neglected the social, experiential side of Christian orthodoxy while we have so overstressed an abstract view of doctrinal orthodoxy as if it could be wholly disconnected from a vibrant living community. In fact, there would be no orthodox ideas without an orthodox community lively enough to sustain itself intergenerationally. From where did the stereotype come? I think from a university ethos where tradition-bashing is the expected thing.

The exhibit made me feel a deep tinge of regret that we Protestants have largely formed our Jewish associations with liberal, culturally accommodative Jews to the neglect of dialogue with conservative and orthodox Jews, thereby missing much of the tough sociological substance of the Jewish experience and contenting ourselves with learning about Judaism only through a thick quasi-Protestantized accommodative lens. Through this lens both the orthodox and the Hassidic Jew have appeared to us as a dated, slightly comic residue of a passing ghetto existence. But, through powerful writers such as Abraham Heschel, Isaac Singer, Eliezer Berkovitz, Emil Fackenheim, and Elie Wiesel, Christian young people are beginning to learn more of the depth and vitality of the orthodox and concervative Jewish experience and even to perceive it as a powerful social model, not only for Jews but for Christians as well.

Orthodox Judaism understands itself to be the authentic conveyor of the tradition that prevailed over virtually the entire Jewish community prior to the emancipation of the eighteenth century. Jewish orthodoxy has placed somewhat less emphasis than Christianity on precise consensual doctrinal definition, and relatively more on submission to the authority of *halakhah* (practice, custom, and oral laws supplementing Torah), but its sociological dynamics are quite similar to Christian orthodoxy, as will be shown. For Jewish orthodoxy looked on any inordinate adjustment of the tradition to the spirit of the time as imcompatible with the *halakhah*. It held that the final norm of human behavior is God's revealed will, not the cultural context in which the

Jewish community might for the moment exist. So orthodox Jews have vigorously resisted ambitious and overweening programs of "reform" that were motivated essentially by an attempt to accommodate the religious community to Enlightenment thinking. It was especially feared that Judaism would be made over into a wordy quasi-Protestant phenomenon of general, secular, modern, ethical consciousness that would amount to an abandonment of the tradition.

Among orthodox Jews, there is no thought of "improving" or "updating" the Torah or adjusting it conveniently to the spirit of the times, but only of seeking to clarify its meaning in the light of ever-changing historical situations. The thornier issue, which has preoccupied a good deal of debate among orthodox Jews, has been whether or to what degree those who cooperate with secular cultural movements can still be regarded as orthodox. This debate has continued into modern Israel, represented by two important stances within orthodox Judaism: the more strictly separationist Agudat Israel, who have frowned on many forms of secular learning, as distinguished from the Mizrachi, who hold to orthodox faith but have been somewhat more sympathetic toward worldly culture. The overarching concern of all orthodox bodies, however, is the maintenance of distinctive Jewish identity within emerging and declining forms of environing cultural expression. The mark of orthodoxy has often been the willingness to forego certain privileges offered by the Emancipation and expanded by modernity in order to sustain that identity. The overriding fear, of course, is of the uncritical assimilation of Jews into modern consciousness.

Just as the theology of orthodoxy requires a concept of heterodoxy, so does the sociology of orthodoxy require the drawing of lines that imply social negation, nonlegitimacy, and corporate rejection. We can see both of these strata, theological and sociological, in orthodox Judaism.

First, on the theological level, we note that several terms were used in the Talmudic and rabbinic literature to refer to heresy or heterodoxy. The Talmudic *min* (heretic, sectarian) was one who denied Israel's chosenness, the oneness of God, or the authority of the rabbis. Another rabbinic term for heresy, *epiquros*, referred to anyone who negated rabbinic authority, turned from the commandments, and denied the

Torah, or whose views were in general "free of restraint."
Among views considered heretical by Maimonides were the
denial of creation *ex nihilo*, the denial of prophesy, divine
revelation, or God's incorporeality. Other authorities extended the term *epiquros* to include any demeaning of the
office of the rabbis. Another term, *kopfer* (a freethinker or
heretic), was used especially for those who delighted in
pointing out supposed contradictions between scriptural
texts. One was considered a *mumar* (one who "changes")
even if he rejected only one commandment of the Torah.
Along such lines was the distinction between orthodoxy and
heterodoxy drawn in rabbinic Judaism.

Various forms of social control and group negation were
developed to express sociologically the lines that were drawn
theologically between orthodoxy and heterodoxy. The treatment of unorthodox *minim* by orthodox Jews ranged from not
sharing meals with them to forms of banning and excommunication. In some times and places, heterodoxy was opposed by
a ban prohibiting marriage or by denying burial rites. Meat
slaughtered by a *min* was forbidden; scrolls transcribed by a
min were barred from use. At times, the *minim* were kept out
of the synagogue on the grounds that they would further
divide the community of faith, jeopardize the inner stability
of the faith, or scandalize the Jewish community before the
surrounding world.

The Jewish and Christian practice of excommunication
goes back at least as far as the Pharisees, Essenes, and Dead
Sea Covenanters, who physically separated from their fellowship those who violated their central tenets. Among sects at
various times regarded by orthodox Judaism as heterodox
were the Samaritans, the Shabbateans (under Shabbetai
Zevi), the followers of Jacob Frank, some devotees of the
Zohar, and adherents of the pantheistic tendencies of Spino-
za. Moses Mendelssohn was chief among modern Jewish
thinkers to argue that all attempts to restrict ideas are self-
defeating and that mistaken notions can be opposed only by
gentle reason, not by coercive actions resulting in separation.

What is postcritical Christian theology learning from Jewish orthodoxy? It is more the learning of a style than a content
and in many ways more a sociological then a theological
learning. It is the discovery of an unapologetic pride and

candor about being faithful guardians of religious tradition precisely amid the conditions of modernity without asking either for modernity's blessing or opinion. It is a willingness to fight and, if necessary, die for the continuity and authenticity of the tradition. It is the joy of dancing with a great historical community to be instructed by Torah and not assuming instant wisdom on the basis of limited, subjective, personal experience. Young Christians who are just beginning to venture into postmodern consciousness with roots in antiquity are learning quickly and profoundly from young Jews who at this point in history have a deeper intuitive sense of what that means.

Is the Question of Heresy Askable?

The leading candidate for "most ugly issue in theology today" is unquestionably heresy. We avoid it like bubonic plague. If we saw someone coming down the street whom we even vaguely suspected might raise the subject of heresy with us, we would find some way of ducking into a hidden place until that person had passed.

Why? Because we are programmed to affable religious permissiveness and the rhetoric of compliance. It is what has been called the "Protestant smile" (John Cuddihy, *Civil Religion and Protestant Taste*). Our least favored interaction pattern as Christian teachers is the role of a harsh judge. We detest judging, unless we happen to be risklessly judging something that is universally condemned by modernity (like militarism, fascism, and old-fashionedness). This is one reason we are not so swift at theology.

Few have shown the courage to draw even the most elementary distinctions between the truth of the Christian faith and that which differs from it. We know that every affirmation implies the negation of its opposite. Since we do not want to be caught negating anything, we do not make any significant affirmations either. I am exaggerating, of course, but the general pattern is a deep malaise in Christian theology, which hungers inordinately for an amiable reputation.

The very word *heresy* turns our minds instantly to terrorizing images of the inquisitions of the sixteenth century and divisive heresy trials of later Protestant sectarianism. Even when we read the careful, closely reasoned anathemas against heresy in the fourth century, we still cannot get the medieval or Puritan witch-hunts out of our minds. The sad history of the subsequent abuses of so-called orthodoxies has created grave obstacles of conscience for us today as we seek even minimally to understand the theological energy that went into precise doctrinal definition in the early Christian period. We tend to see the question of heresy only through modern lenses that fixate on the abuses of medieval and Counter-Reformation political authority and Puritan hysteria, so as to distort our perception of the intricate mosaic of earlier Christian doctrinal definition.

Sometimes the sobering history of repressions against heresy makes us wonder if the church's legitimate struggle to define itself by negation has been perennially prone to pride and excess. The effect of the Thirty Years' War (1616–48) and the periods of severe persecution both by and against Protestants has made heresy a dreaded term among dissenting parties ever since the sixteenth century. The civil abuses against heretics remain heavy on the conscience of both Catholics and Protestants. So anyone who risks digging up the thorny question of heresy must be willing to learn from the checkered history of its abuse. To make good on this commitment, Christians today must be willing to work as hard as anyone to preserve political toleration for unpopular religious views. We can best do penance for a witch-hunting history by offering vigorous civil protection to those threatened by contemporary witch-hunters.

The emotional inflammability of the question of heresy might be calmed by an unhurried reflection on the ancient meaning of the term. The idea of *hairesis* emerged early in the Christian tradition out of the cauldron of apostasy. It simply meant self-choice—from *hairein* (to take) and *haireisthai* (to choose for oneself)—hence an alternative self-chosen view, as opposed to apostolic teaching as interpreted by ecumenical consensus. *Hairesis* was an attachment to some teaching "other than" the delivered tradition, with some consequent disruption of the church's unity and continuity. This is why *hairesis* in the New Testament is so often

associated with a divisive party spirit, a disruptive factional-
ism that was willing callously to strike out at the always
vulnerable unity and catholicity of the church. It was in its
struggle to conserve the delivered tradition and defend it
from challenges that the early church found it necessary to
develop duly accredited channels for the teaching authority
of the church as expressed through the offices of *episkopos*
and *presbuteros*. From their inception, these offices of
ministry have been charged with guardianship of the authenticity of the apostolic witness within their limited, local or
regional sphere of responsibility. The *hairesis* against which
they were charged to defend the church was not just any
miscellaneous opinion, but rather any *heteran pistin*, any
contravening faith or any opinion contrary to apostolic
teaching.

When Paul learned that the Galatians were quickly turning
away to a "different gospel" than the mercy of Christ, he
wrote them that there is no other gospel than "that which you
received" (Gal. 1:9 RSV). "Even if we, or an angel from
heaven, should preach to you a gospel contrary to that which
we preached to you, let him be accursed" (Gal. 1:8 RSV). The
truth of Paul's message was not, in his view, to be judged
even by his personal authority or prophetic gifts, but solely by
whether it was true to the standard of the apostolic teaching
(1 Cor. 15:1–3). He exhorted his readers in Rome to "keep
your eye on those who stir up quarrels and lead others astray,
contrary to the teaching you received" (Rom. 16:17). The
awareness of heresy that we find early in Paul we find
expanded many times in later New Testament sources. So to
imagine heresy essentially as a post-New Testament problem
is a gross misconception.

We have never had a church that had no difficulties with
heresy, in the sense of exemption from the struggle with
challenging alternatives to the delivered tradition. In fact, a
good case can be made that all the current heresies are
essentially reformulations of the early ones familiar to the first
five centuries.

Paul agreed that there is a hidden, provident reason why
heresy exists so persistently among Christian communities:
namely, "dissensions are necessary if only to show which of
your members are sound" (1 Cor. 11:19). Heresy is permitted

by the grace of God in order that the true faith may be reflected in the light of its false expressions.

Heresy does not just involve personal doubt or denial; it also must be understood sociologically, as a challenge to the unity and continuity of the community of faith. Among the "deeds of the flesh" that Paul associated with the heretical spirit were "quarrels, a contentious temper, envy, fits of rage, selfish ambitions, dissensions, party intrigues" (Gal. 5:20).

Heresy does not come as a challenge from some source outside the church, but from within it, in which some dimension of Christian truth is overemphasized to the neglect of the balance and wholeness found in the delivered, consensually received apostolic-canonical tradition. So Ebionism was an overcompensated attempt to conserve the humanity of Jesus at the expense of his divinity, and Docetism was an excessive attempt in the other direction to stress his divine origin at the expense of neglecting his humanity and actual suffering.

Some readers of recent theology have come routinely to expect theology to be looking for "something different" all the time. They have an insatiable hunger for "alternative approaches," "new visions," and supposed "radical departures" in theology. These terms come very close to being a rough translation of what the church fathers called *heterodoxy*. Canon VII of the Council of Ephesus provided that it is canonically unlawful "to compose a different [*heteran*] faith as a rival to that established by the holy Fathers assembled with the Holy Spirit in Nicaea." Chalcedon decreed that no one shall be allowed to "bring forward a different faith" (*heteran pistin*) or a "different creed" (*heteron symbolon*).

The intent of the council fathers was not to prohibit the enlargement of our understanding of the faith, but only the fabrication of teachings contrary to the faith once delivered to the saints. One of the commonest definitions of heresy in the early church was "that which we have invented" in contrast to "that which we have received." Yet the mainstream of recent theology persists in thinking of its fundamental task as that of doctrinal innovation, modernization, and supposed improvement on the embarrassingly "dated" faith of our ancient ecumenical foremothers and forefathers. It is to all who hold this opinion that this minority report is respectfully addressed.

Orthodoxy stands in an intrinsic relation with heresy. Orthodoxy seeks to clarify the difference between the apostolic teaching of Jesus Christ and other views (*hairesis*). Insofar as that distinction is abandoned, Christian teaching is enervated and immobilized. Where there is no distinction between Christian truth and falsehood parading as Christian truth, there can be no Christian teaching.

Orthodoxy as Theological Method

By "theological method," theologians usually mean the ground rules by which theology is supposed to proceed. Debates on theological method often come down to the question of authority: What kinds of statements are to be admitted in discourse about God, and on what authority?

Christian orthodoxy of the first Christian millennium proceeded with a consensual theological method grounded in historical revelation. Theology speaks of the triune God on the basis of the eventful self-disclosure of God in history. These events are made known in Scripture, rigorously reflected upon by reason, and experienced personally through a living liturgical tradition. Faith seeks an understanding of itself in each new cultural context. Christian social experience has shown that private, individual experiences and reasonings need the constant guidance of Scripture and tradition in order to be animated wholesomely by the revelation of God in universal history, in the people of Israel, and in Jesus Christ. Far from denying or neglecting reason and experience, orthodoxy wishes to embody them in and through a living tradition. Accordingly, reason and experience rise to their higher possibilities only in response to grace. Orthodoxy sought to identify the consensus that has prevailed among those who received the apostolic testimony concerning God's revelation.

I am proposing in this agenda a return to the normative self-restrictions that prevailed in Christianity's first millennium. But why the first millennium? Not because this period was intrinsically more exciting than other eras, or its advocates more brilliant, but because of its close adherence to apostolic faith and because a more complete ecumenical consensus was achieved in that period than any period since, a consensus that in fact has been subsequently affirmed by Protestant, Catholic, and Orthodox traditions.

If the second Christian millennium ends in a denial of the first Christian millennium, it will amount to a denial of its own history and to a radical splitting in two of its identity. The task of postcritical orthodoxy is to restore consensual primitive ecumenism. The task is to rediscover what makes Christians of the late twentieth century spiritually more like Christians of the fifth or fifteenth century than like admired persons of one's own hometown or family who have not heard and believed God's Good News. Part of the joy of historical discovery in Christianity is the growing awareness of this affinity with persons who lived in very different cultural periods than we live in, whose faith was shaped by lively participation in Christ, whose love remains the same yesterday, today, and forever.

The thrust of orthodox theological method is seen in its own statements about why the councils were convened: not to "remove the ancient landmarks" but to "remain steadfast in the testimonies and authority of the holy and approved fathers" (Third Council of Constantinople); to "drive away the laughter of the heterodox" (Chalcedon); to "unite the churches again and to bring the Synod of Chalcedon together with the three earlier, to universal acceptance." "We hold that faith which our Lord Jesus Christ, the true God, delivered to his holy apostles, and through them to the holy churches, and which they who after them were holy fathers and doctors, handed down to the people committed to them" (Second Council of Constantinople). The precise focus was on accurate transmission, not innovation. The council fathers were especially sensitive to points at which the faith was under attack: "Let us be in all things of one mind, of one heart, when the faith, which is one, is attacked. Let the whole body grieve and mourn in common with us" (Council of Ephesus).

Later Luther, despite his reputation as a reforming disrupter of consensus, instructed his pastors to "avoid changes or variations in the text" of liturgy or catechism: "Adopt one form, adhere to it, and use it repeatedly year after year. [For people] are easily confused if a teacher employs one form now and another form—perhaps with the intention of making improvements—later on."

The theological method of orthodoxy proceeds not by asking how we feel or about which theologian's view is most brilliant or about probability estimates of success or about whether the faith can adjust itself to various worldviews, but rather it proceeds by pursuing a simple question relentlessly: What in fact did the apostles teach? The same question put differently: What is the baptism into which we have been baptized? Taken seriously, this question simplifies the theological effort considerably, sharpens the focus, and hedges against diversions. After hearing the Tome of Leo, the fathers at Chalcedon cried out, "This is the faith of the fathers, this is the faith of the Apostles. So we all believe, thus the orthodox believe." They intuited it, knew it, remembered it, and tested it by its correspondence with the apostolic teaching.

"It is not necessary that traditions and ceremonies be in all places one, or utterly like," the Anglican Thirty-nine Articles wisely affirmed, "for at all times they have been diverse, and may be changed according to the diversity of countries, times, and . . . manners." The same article gently chides the intemperate spirit who irascibly breaks church traditions even when they are not in conflict with Scriptures, since such iconoclasm injures respect for authority generally and "wounds the conscience of the weak brethren." In the relatively tolerant central tradition of Anglican orthodoxy, we see a wise balance of grace and freedom, apostolicity and cultural imagination, doctrinal firmness yet tolerant respect for the variety of social traditions. The English church tradition happily embraced this tolerant pluralism and then shipped it to America, where it has borne delicious fruits. Yet in its liberalizing and pietistic American forms, it has tended to lose the rich liturgical and doctrinal center that had been the beacon light to previous radically experimenting generations.

Can the theological method of ancient ecumenical orthodoxy be directly and straightforwardly adopted by postcritical Christian classicism? Probably not directly, but its intention stands as a significant corrective to the distortions we have been experiencing. For it wishes more than anything to have a good, clear memory. It understands itself to be charged with the care of the apostolic tradition. It responds to ever new challenges, guided by ancient ecumenical consensus as it was led by the Holy Spirit. Orthodoxy does not search for a consensus of current opinion, but for the apostolic consensus that itself had been repeatedly reaffirmed and defined by the previous ecumenical councils, and that had repeatedly challenged and transformed emerging modernities.

When we penetrate the façades, we often find that the liberal Protestant minister has a hidden orthodox side and a revealed modern side. We enjoy displaying the public liberal face and posture. Deep inside us, somehow, is the quiet appropriation within our personality structure of the apostolic tradition and Trinitarian Christian orthodoxy. The Christological images in the hymns of the church are mixed in the marrow of our bones. Protestant worshiping communities have received the *consensus fidelium* more through hymns, prayers, and liturgies than through preaching, where we have a right to expect it. The scriptural metaphors resonate quietly in our modern consciousness and memory even when we are trying to put on an up-to-date face. They tell us who we are, revealing to us the depths of our lostness, our moral situation before God that we neglect to the detriment of our souls.

We know all this. How strange it is, then, that we so easily put down that side of ourselves, deny it, disavow it, do not let it be. Scratch the surface of the average Protestant pastor and find that underneath the public, calculatedly nonprudish, "no offense," "liberated" side that smiles awkwardly about sex and frowns with concern about pollution, there remains a hunger for the clear proclamation of God's radical, saving, judging love for humanity in Jesus Christ, the risen and living Lord, and an awareness of the holy God present in our midst to judge our idolatries and forgive our sins. An orthodox heart beats quietly behind a permissive smile.

We see also the limitations of orthodoxy: its temptation, despite its best intuitions, to view all reality from a limited vantage point; its intolerances and inequalities; its pretense and pride. But at its heart, we know that classical Christianity is wiser and better than its modern alternatives. Many of us born of Protestant liberalism have expended enormous energies trying to flee the claims of orthodoxy. Liberalism is a tradition against tradition. We have been through a long negative-reinforcement training process to teach us a kind of general distrust of orthodoxy. Somewhere deep inside, however, we know that we do not have anything better to offer, and that our experimentations depend upon the larger frame of reference in which to experiment, which orthodoxy has nurtured and protected.

12

The Faith
Once Delivered

It seems obvious to most believers that there is a solemn pastoral duty to teach and defend correct Christian doctrine. They think the unifying center of the tradition is evident. They know that outrageous denials of Christian truth should not go unchallenged, especially when taught by one specifically ordained and authorized to defend Christian teaching. So what is the fuss about, and what is the point of making an agenda item for something everyone already knows?

The problem is that this pastoral duty has not been vigorously pursued. The unifying center has not been sufficiently defined. The ancient heresies flourish in every quarter unrecognized as such, often baptized and blessed by the parson's affable smile. After all, who needs controversy; and don't forget, the membership rolls could easily suffer from such probing questions.

Many tolerant liberal churchmen have a knee-jerk negative reaction to almost any talk of God's will, revelation, or providence or the Trinity, not to mention atonement, redemption, and divine judgment. Many fall sociologically into an independent, nonaligned, unaffiliated, unchurched category. Among these are professors of religion who may look with disdain on most institutional Christianity and seldom participate in its Eucharist, yet feel that they can with complete adequacy evaluate Christian doctrine and even stand as fully accredited teachers of Christian religion. On cue they are happy to present their advanced degree in religious studies from a major modern university spawned by a mainline denomination.

I am not describing a situation that does not exist. Unfortunately, it exists virtually unchecked by significant rational criticism or caveats, except those that can be discounted as coming from the right tip of the right wing. This situation has emerged because our own Protestant tradition has been sloppy in housekeeping and in reasonably monitoring its own criteria for ordination and teaching.

Meanwhile, the faithful laity have assumed that the teaching office would be properly secured and accountable to the original message of Christianity. They have relied on their ordained ministry. As one who has spent his professional life in schools that educate ordained ministers, I cannot in good conscience say that the faith and hope of the laity in the teaching office has on the whole been justified. That, if true, should be a special burden of conscience on all of us who share the teaching office. It is our responsibility to guarantee our own professional standards no less than physicians or lawyers or nuclear waste disposal officials or building contractors must guarantee theirs. When we fail to speak out against evident abuses or fail to challenge outrageous offenses against Christian teaching, the whole body suffers.

If we care about the authenticity and clarity of the church's teaching, can we remain passive in the face of out-and-out heterodox challenges to faith when they appear in our own specific sphere of responsibility and masquerade as authentic Christian teaching? Every pastor has to make situational judgments about when and where to respond to heretical teaching as it emerges, but few pastors of conscience do not struggle with this problem in some profound way. What worries me is that theology of late has provided very little assistance in this practical struggle to maintain the genuineness of Christian teaching in the local setting. Is it so scandalous to hope that ordained ministers would represent the apostolic teaching accurately or that lay Christian teachers should receive competent instruction in Christian doctrine? Don't hold your breath awaiting an answer. One might think such questions would be answered routinely, but the fact is that they contain volatile issues that do not admit of easy settlement.

This places us unexpectedly on the creative edge of the ecumenical movement today, regrettably mired in demoralization and identity confusion. The unity of the body of Christ exists already in Christ, but we manifest it miserably in our institutional structures. It may be that the enriching of the church's unity in our time will occur only at the stiff cost of a certain purification of the church's teaching. We have brushed under our ecumenical rugs so many ancient heresies that our rugs now bulge in the middle. You may protest that the facing of questions so volatile as heresy will be divisive and thus will create in tranquil churches the very disruption that we associate with heresy itself. My experience in working with adult Christian laypersons leads me to believe that what they want and expect most from their ordained ministry is that it will deliver to them genuine Christian teaching and be able to distinguish it from the counterfeits. The risk of divisiveness is a necessary risk worth taking. If the term *purification* is too scary, could we at least agree that advocacy of classical Christian teaching within the framework of the open pursuit of the truth must remain a possibility within every Christian congregation and college and church agency? Does that sound like an easy agreement? Don't bet on it.

Quality Control: Who Is in Charge?

The most avoided issue of contemporary theological controversy has been *hairesis*. It is precisely because it has been ignored for several generations, that it has become all the more necessary for the emerging generation to face up to it.

The judicatories often seem unwilling or unable to oversee doctrinal teaching in their own areas or dioceses. Superintendents of ministers and judicatory officials often do not exercise any effective control over the quality of Christian teaching in their areas. I have made cautious inquiries among several denominations. Businesses have quality control on their products, but in Christian teaching, important as it is, there seems to be a marked absence of quality control. Some, of course, prefer that it remain minimal.

Those who look to the seminaries for theological quality control indeed have a right to expect it, but they should look realistically at the sociology of professionalization in theology today before they expect a quick turnaround. There are good reasons to doubt whether the seminaries with their present predilections are even prepared to grasp, much less solidly pursue, the problem. If not the seminaries or regional judicatories, then who is minding the store? The task will fall, as usual, mainly on the working pastor.

The Christian community has always been aware that God the Spirit has providentially cared for its continuity amid hazardous environments. Hence theology at its best has had no reason to approach its subject matter—God—with intense anxiety or despair. It is not up to us finally to guarantee the continuity of the tradition, except in our own small and specific range of responsibility; but within that range it is up to us, especially among those who are ordained and authorized to teach, to whom the teaching office is solemnly entrusted.

For the faith to be delivered to each new cultural setting, each succeeding generation must come to grips with the original apostolic witness. Easy substitutes and glossy reinterpretations won't do. When one generation fails, that makes it ever so much more difficult for the immediately succeeding generation. But, if it is elementary to the very definition of the church that it exists in time, it therefore must be a tradition and thus must understand itself as an intergenerational process. There is no nonhistorical shortcut to fulfilling once for all the church's mission, no easy way to accomplish all at once, on behalf of every generation, that task of the church, any more than there is a way for Judaism to accomplish its task in a single generation and divest itself ever thereafter of the burden of tradition-maintenance.

We have learned in modernity to keep fashionably silent about the incarnation, atonement, and resurrection and to develop theological positions less controversial and more agreeable with the assumptions of modernity—that Jesus is a good teacher (with minimal "mythological" additions), that God is good, but would not dare to judge our iniquities, and so on. In only one century of focusing on the ethical relevance of Jesus' teaching, we have almost forgotten how to speak of and pray to Jesus Christ, the Son of God and Savior of the world. In the well-intentioned attempt to deliver the Christian message in a language acceptable to moderns, we have peeled the onion almost down to nothing. We have cheated our young people out of the hard but necessary Christian word about human sin and divine redemption.

This has put us in a self-alienated situation. When we divorce Christian morality from its ground in divine grace, Christianity becomes a pathetic, almost laughable example of this religious contradiction: a highly intensified idealism that systematically cuts itself off from the energy that would make possible the fulfillment of that idealism. The power of the Christian life is rooted in the love of God who becomes flesh in Jesus Christ, without whom the radical ideals of the Christian life only tend to make us more guilty and miserable.

Christianity has perennially been challenged to respond to hostile disputants from without. But the political regimes and tyrannies of mind and spirit from without have often been more manageable than the disavowal of faith from within our own household, enunciated in high-sounding terms by those who understand themselves to be doing us some huge favor. So it is not surprising that, from the Pastoral Epistles to the eighteenth century, careful attention has been given to guaranteeing the authenticity of the teaching office of the church.

"No other foundation can any one lay," wrote Paul to the disputatious Corinthians, "than that which is laid, which is Jesus Christ" (1 Cor. 3:11 RSV). The foundation, strictly speaking, is not just Scripture or tradition but Jesus Christ himself, who is the heart of Scripture and tradition, whose mission to many generations requires both canonical Scripture and diligent tradition-maintenance.

At What Point Do the Remedies for Heterodoxy Become More Hazardous Than Heterodoxy Itself?

A cautious caveat: All our historical experience argues against the divisive, judgmental format of the heresy trial. It intensifies animosity and further polarizes positions that might otherwise be reconcilable through persuasion and dialogue. It divides the body of Christ. The circus atmosphere tends less toward procedural fairness than toward self-righteousness, harshness, embitterment. To those possessed by the anxious thought that the trend of this argument might wind up in a recurrent round of ecclesiastical trials, I answer no. Why not, then, and what are the alternatives?

Anyone who launches out in the hazardous territory of our present subject matter (sensitively learning to draw the boundary between heterodoxy and orthodoxy) should recognize a self-defeating psychological dynamic that accompanies the format of the ecclesiastical trial: Everyone loses. The victor in the conflict often comes off looking either like a tyrant or a malcontent. The loser gets the juicy role of innocent victim. The adversary situation is made for journalistic voyeurism, which is always happier to advertise scandal than take note of concurrence or consensual harmony. The more outrageous the views under discussion, the more the media interest will gain sharp focus.

The preferred alternative to a coercive, adversary format is the ancient tradition of pastoral admonition and confidential spiritual counsel. This pattern is already well established in the New Testament, which centers far more attention on the gentle admonition of false teachers than on the courtroom paradigm. The corrective concern is focused less on laypersons than on teachers; less on coercion than on persuasion. Similarly today, where flagrant heterodox teaching repeatedly occurs among those who have solemnly received the credentials and commission of ordination by a duly authorized church body that has approved their competence to teach Christian doctrine, the remedy of that body rightly will begin with gentle admonition, coupled with a clear biblical rationale for the interests of the community in the truth of Christian teaching.

Is it too much to ask or hope that some judicatories or bishops or credentials committees or boards of ministry will have the courage on occasion to inquire about alleged flagrant abuses of the teaching office? Or if, after serious and fair examination, the fulmination against Christian doctrine should continue, would it not then be reasonable for a judicatory to ask the teacher to show cause why the credential should be continued, or how the person might properly be supervised or pastorally advised in the interest of the Christian community? Such questions open a Pandora's box.

Pastoral admonition does well to proceed with scrupulous concern for due process, fairness, and the protection of the legitimate rights of all. "But," you may ask, "at what point does pastoral admonition constitute an infringement of civil rights or academic freedom?" Keep in mind that ordination is not a civil right; it is an ecclesiastical office solemnly covenanted to preach the Word faithfully. The question of whether one is fulfilling one's obligation to church teaching is indeed a contractual question, but its adjudication lies strictly within the realm of ecclesial, not civil, judgment; for no civil law can decide what is correct religious teaching. That is quite beyond the competence of civil authority.

On the same grounds, there can and must be no punishment for heterodox teaching other than simply withholding the religious body's approval or permission to preach. That cannot be an offense against a civil right, because the ordination to preach is not a civil right. If in some future time a court should overextend its authority so as to dictate to a religious body how it is to monitor the authenticity of its own teaching, that would be a clear violation of religious liberty and such interference should be resolutely resisted by civil rights advocates.

Polemics and Irenics: Neglected Frontier Disciplines?

In an intense discussion with colleagues on curriculum, I testily suggested that what today's seminary most needs is a polemicist, trained in the rough-and-tumble give and take of old-fashioned scholastic Protestant polemics. They chided me patiently and challenged me to write an advertisement for the *Chronicle of Higher Education* that might attract a good polemicist; so I did:

HELP WANTED: Christian polemicist. Ph.D. Must be courageous, honest, and thoroughly schooled both in the exacting logic of orthodoxy and the sciences of modernity; intelligent, witty, committed, tough; hard as nails in public debate, but with a warm heart and human touch; must be able to sharpen with precision the fine theological distinctions that modern audiences often find irritating and difficult to grasp, yet make them clear and as interesting to us as they have been for the ancients. Must be morally incorruptible and willing to die for the cause. We are an equal opportunity employer.

The irony of such an announcement lies not in its content but in the fact that it would be utterly unthinkable that any respected university or seminary would even consider actually placing such an ad or making a search for such a polemics-person.

Doctrinal definition is as essential to the task of theology as identifying a phony dollar bill is to the job of a bank teller. To define is to set a boundary (Latin *definire*: "to limit, mark out, set bounds"). Yet we have been trying to practice the art of theology while studiously avoiding the embarrassing task of setting any boundaries.

Keep in mind, however, that there can be no definition of anything without excluding from that definition that which is different from it. In fact, that is precisely the definition of *definition*. And so it is with doctrinal definition.

Polemics is that traditional branch of Christian theology, now having lain fallow for several decades, that has sought to identify the proper boundaries of Christian belief and to distinguish the apostolic teaching from its counterfeits and alternatives. It is a border-defining discipline. As courts and realtors rely on a surveyor to say precisely "Here is the boundary," so has theology in the past sought the advice of an academic specialist called polemicist to say "Here marks the exact line that distinguishes false from true Christian teaching." Yet we in theology today have preferred to do a booming business in religious real estate without any surveyor at all.

Suppose one is trying scrupulously to determine whether a particularly volatile, avowedly Marxist national revolutionary party is "genuinely Marxist" or not? Would not all claimants instantly appeal to the classical texts of Marxism in order to settle such a dispute? Wouldn't the authenticity or doctrinal orthodoxy of subsequent schismatic spinoffs of later Marxism reasonably be assessed in relation to what Marx himself and other early theorists had said, and not the other way around?

But in recent theology we have turned this procedure on its head by assuming that "modern man" must self-evidently be the final and absolute arbiter of the authenticity of Christian doctrine, and if certain phrases of the Council of Ephesus do not fit into our modern assumptions, we feel perfectly justified in blue-lining them out of our fantasies about "genuine Christianity."

The sister discipline that once neatly complemented and toned down polemics was irenics, from the lovely Greek word for peaceful, *eirenikos*. While polemics tried to mark out the borders of Christianity, irenics talked about the conditions for peace within the borders. While polemics tried precisely to identify the forms of the *dissensus* falling between faith and unfaith, irenics looked for the deeper forms of consensus within the community of faith. Irenic theology is conciliatory, reconciling, and peacemaking within the boundaries of the delivered apostolic tradition. Melanchthon, Bucer, and Cranmer are sixteenth-century prototypes of irenic orthodoxy. Leo the Great, Vincent of Lérins, Thomas Aquinas, and Nicholas of Cusa would represent the irenic spirit in the earlier tradition. Modern irenics reached its apex in the nineteenth century with the great works of comparative symbolics by J. A. Moehler, Philipp Marheinecke, Ferdinand Kattenbusch, G. F. Oehler, and Charles Briggs, but from there on it was all downhill. It quickly became lost in the shuffle of twentieth-century impulses toward token and surface ecumenism.

Irenics now awaits rediscovery and redevelopment as a theological and historical discipline. Its guiding principle then and now remains the ancient formula of Rupertus Meldenius that became so widely quoted later by Protestants: "*In necessariis, unitas; in non necessariis, libertas; in utrisque, caritas*" ("in essentials, unity, in nonessentials liberty, in all things charity").

Polemical orthodoxy without irenic orthodoxy is combative and overly aggressive; irenics without polemics is borderless and diffuse. A postcritical irenics will concern itself with the cohesive center of the tradition, while an alert, adept, creative, postcritical polemical orthodoxy will concern itself with the circumference and try accurately and in good spirit to monitor the boundaries. Each of these disciplines needs the other, and both are urgently needed today. But they are lost arts, and their recovery is a crucial agenda item for theology today.

13

The Center of a Wide Circumference

My teacher, H. Richard Niebuhr, was fond of quoting F. D. Maurice that most of us are right in what we affirm and wrong in what we deny. The preceding argument has required such a combative spirit that one might assume that such a wise maxim had been long repudiated. But, because I believe it is true, it is now time for me to redress the legitimate grievance of the reader who might think I have only relentless negations to offer and no positive agenda. So this chapter is offered as a modest constructive initiative in the form of a proposal for debate.

After all, an agenda does not in itself finally settle issues— that is what happens in the parliamentary process. It rather only proposes the crucial issues to be discussed. So, even if I do not work fully through the issue of this chapter concerning whether the central continuity of the Christian tradition can be defined, I would at least hope to be convincing that this is the unavoidable theological issue we must thoroughly debate in the last decade of the twentieth century. The writing of a systematic theology is necessary fully to develop these implications. That is just what I have been doing the last several years.

There is a touch of comic incongruity in the realization that after almost two thousand years of debate we are still not sure what Christianity *is* and still have royal battles as to whether it is even definable. It was W. R. Matthews who quipped that it seems even "more difficult to discover what Christianity is than to believe it when it is discovered."

The opposite point was more persuasively made by Kierkegaard, however, in his parable of the $100,000 gift, that we understand all too well *what* Christianity is but rather have to take extreme measures to protect ourselves against its rigorous claims:

> Suppose that it was said in the New Testament—we can surely suppose it—that it is God's will that every man should have 100,000 dollars: Do you think there would be any question of a commentary? Or would not everyone rather say, "It's easy enough to understand, there's no need of a commentary, let us for heaven's sake keep clear of commentaries—they could perhaps make it doubtful whether it is really as it is written. (And with their help we even run the risk that it may become doubtful.) But we prefer it to be as it stands written there, so away with all commentaries!"

> But what is found in the New Testament (about the narrow way, dying to the world, and so on) is not at all more difficult to understand than this matter of the 100,000 dollars. The difficulty lies elsewhere, in that it does not please us—and so we must have commentaries and professors and commentaries; for it is not a case of "risking" that it may become doubtful to us, for we really wish it to be doubtful, and we have a tiny hope that the commentaries may make it so (Kierkegaard, *The Last Years*, 334–35).

The Spectrum

The key proposal of this chapter is that the circle of the Christian tradition has an unusually wide circumference without ceasing to have a single, unifying center. It is Christ's living presence that unites a diverse tradition, yet that single center is experienced in richly different ways. Christ's presence is experienced sacramentally by the liturgical traditions, spiritually by the charismatic traditions, as morally inspiring by the liberal traditions, as ground of social experiment by the pietistic traditions, as doctrinal teacher by the scholastic traditions, as sanctifying power of persons and society by the Greek Orthodox tradition, as grace perfecting nature by the Roman Catholic tradition, and as word of

Scripture by the evangelical tradition. All of these traditions and the periods of their hegemony have experienced the living and risen Christ in spectacularly varied ways. But nothing else than the living Christ forms the center of this wide circumference.

The varieties of the tradition may be viewed as if Christ were a spectral prism through which God's love is refracted on the changing surfaces of the evoluting world. The lens creates a burst of vibrant colors. It breaks up a single beam of light and reveals all the variety of colors already implicitly within that beam. Christ is the lens. The study of the tradition is like looking through a magnificent spectroscope. The colors are strikingly different, just as Christian perceptions of the living Christ have been abundantly diverse. There is no boredom in the subject. It is as if in certain periods, Christianity has become enamored with soft pastels and aquas, while in another century gaudy iridescent oranges or mellow oyster whites might have captured its imagination. Yet the same unchanging, steadfast love of God in Christ is variably manifested in the entire polychromatic scale. Seen together historically, they manifest the full rainbow of God's presence in the estranged world.

It therefore becomes mean and restrictive to assume testily that only one color finally *is* the most beautiful or permanently normative for all the rest. Furthermore, because history is not completed, we need not assume that we have already seen all possible tonal nuances of Christian orthodoxy. We indeed have a basic and full spectrum of colors in the faith of the early saints and martyrs, but it has taken the tradition many centuries to discover, examine, and explicitly savor certain shades and tints. This is why the study of church history and historical theology has an especial aesthetic appeal at this juncture of cultural history, because it is like a catalogue of colors of Christian self-actualization.

When we hear the language of orthodoxy echoing in our modern minds, we are sometimes tempted to say to ourselves that surely we could have stated it better than that! It appears antiquated, narrow, and harsh at best, and at worst, immoral, nationalistic, triumphalist, or presumptuous. In those moments it is difficult to find the historical empathy necessary to listen carefully to the earliest creeds and symbols speak from within their own nexus of historical challenges and with the particular linguistic and philosophical resources they had available at hand to them.

Yet when we begin nondefensively listening, we sense a tremendously creative process in orthodoxy's active engagement with the cultural challenges it has faced. It has moved imaginatively through and beyond gnosticism, the mystery religions, neo-Platonism, Manichaeanism, stoicism, Aristotelianism, nominalism, and many sociocultural languages, right on down to contemporary empiricism, existentialism, Marxism, and deconstructionism, transmuting each one of them along the way. But these changing valences do not in themselves constitute an explanation of the center that makes the varied tradition unified. The identification of that center is a major assignment of the agenda for theology today, of which this discussion can only be a preliminary anticipation.

The Vital Center

Obviously, Christianity has undergone many cultural transformations, just as has Jewish consciousness. But where is the scarlet thread that runs through all these changes? What persistently underlies all these curious mutations in Christian consciousness? The answer to that question would be the core of the tradition, the cohesive pattern, the center of the circumference, that which makes the Christian tradition finally a single tradition, not merely a legion of independent, absorptive, cultural accommodations. Hence the question cannot be rightly raised while at the same time ignoring the historical varieties of Christianity.

Surely there must be many ways, not just one, to articulate this center, because Christianity has passed through so many symbol systems and worldviews. Whenever Christianity seriously has approached a new cultural formation, however, it has always found itself decisively instructed by returning to the most primitive attempts of ancient ecumenical Christianity to define its center. That usually has meant not only canonical Scripture but early Christian doctrinal definitions and symbolic confessions, such as the Apostles' and Nicaea-

Constantinopolitan creeds, widely respected as perennially valuable approaches to the core.

It is an elementary point in logic that something can have unity only if it has variety. Unity is by definition a concord of related yet different parts. That which has no variety cannot be said to have any definite sort of unity.

So it is with Christian orthodoxy, that it has transgenerational unity in Christ only because it has luxuriant varieties in history. It would be comic to speak solemnly about some orthodox unity unless there were in fact a genuine variety of cultural expressions of orthodoxy. It is on the basis of this premise that we speak of still one more emerging variety of orthodoxy—postcritical. A new tonal texture, a delicate new shade is forming from the same source of spectral light that has manifested itself otherwise in other times and places.

It was this question that initiated a shift in my consciousness: Might it be that it is *only* when we richly behold the vast historical varieties of the orthodox tradition that we are finally able to grasp something of the central thread running quietly through all its flux? It is something like a visual puzzle that one can only recognize through much looking, standing back, and turning the picture at an angle, seeing it finally as a simple gestalt precisely through its awesome complexities.

This reminded me of a startling image from Kierkegaard's Quidam in *States on Life's Way*: "When an examining magistrate has perhaps been sitting for a long time reading documents, hearing testimony, confronting witnesses, exploring localities—just as he sits there in the chamber he suddenly sees something. It is not a man, a new witness, it is not the *corpus delicti*, it is a something, and he calls it 'the course of events.' As soon as he sees the course of events, he, the examiner, has all he wants" (Kierkegaard, *Stages on Life's Way*, 288). Suppose it is precisely in looking intently *through* the profuse varieties of Christian orthodoxy that we can begin to grasp with simplicity what holds it all together. What follows is merely my own impression of this "course of events" that enables us to grasp the unifying vitality of the varied tradition.

The fact that the tradition keeps on trying to identify its center supports the primary intuition that some vital center necessarily exists. I do not want to put heavy emphasis, however, on what I personally would wish the center to be, or what I think, by current public opinion analysis, a majority or plurality of modern Christians might think it to be. Rather, it must be defined by asking historically: To what has the tradition itself through its liturgy, pastoral care, and confessions persistently pointed as the center of its vitality? Stated in that way, the center of the tradition should not in principle be regarded as mysterious or ineffable, for Christian preaching seeks constantly to articulate it even though preaching is aware that it is using mutable languages and fragile, changing symbol systems.

When we listen carefully to the tradition speak of itself, here is the primary pattern that expresses itself in the mosaic of Christian liturgies and texts: The center of the tradition is *life in Christ*. Christianity is distinctive as a religious faith in that it understands itself (both originally and in the present time) to be living as a continuing community through the living Christ.

Christianity is not unique in understanding itself to have been founded by a particular historical person, for Islam and Buddhism both share that feature. Yet Muhammad exists in an entirely different relation to Islam than Jesus does to Christianity; so also Gautama is to Buddhism not at all the same as Jesus is to Christianity. Without diminishing the significance of these companion religions, it is important for us to grasp the difference: it is the resurrected presence of the living Lord that continues to be the sole basis of the present reality of the church. Jesus is not merely the one who founded the community and left it, but rather the one who is present to the community now and in each historical period as the vital essence, the animating, awakening life of the church.

If the central contribution of Jesus to Christianity were his moral instruction or religious insight (as some forms of liberalism taught) or his establishing a sociologically visible religious community (as some sociologies of religion have maintained), one could more easily speak of structural parallels between Christianity, Islam, and Buddhism. But Jesus' importance to the Christian community is misjudged if seen essentially on the level of his moral or religious teaching or organizational ability or conceptual ideas or even, strictly speaking, his own past life. Rather, it focuses on his present life as vitalizing center of the community of faith. This is what is celebrated in Holy Communion: the crucified and resurrected Christ not as a projection of faith but as that to which faith exists as a response. This is what unifies Catholics, charismatics, and traditional Protestants: The Christ of the liturgy is the Christ of the written Word, who is the Christ of the gifts of the Spirit.

The authority of Christ is the sole basis on which all other ecclesiastic authority lies in classical Christianity. Scripture is authoritative essentially because it witnesses to Christ. But Christ is far more than an authority for the church. Much more—Christ is the reality of the church. It is his presence that makes it cohere. Where the living Christ is not present, there the church is not present, at least according to its classical reasoning about itself. Christianity never tires of reminding us of this. Christ is the Way, the Truth, the Life, the Light, the living Word, the Shepherd. Christ is misunderstood as merely the one who points the way. He *is* the Way.

Interpersonal Encounter with the Living Christ

So what is the unifying center of the variegated traditions? The experienced presence of the risen Christ in the midst of the worshiping community. There is no Christian tradition without some form of interpersonal encounter with the living Christ, however variable that encounter may appear in the many languages, cultures, and worldviews of two Christian millennia. Christ remains perennially engaged in the life of the world now as in the first century: "I am with you always," Jesus said to his disciples, "to the end of time" (Matt. 28:20).

However different Augustine's language may be from Luther's, or Thomas Aquinas's from Schleiermacher's, or Nicaea from the Augsburg Confession, they do not differ in the slightest on this central point: that Christianity owes its existence then and now to the continued presence of the person of Christ even amid the most drastic historical reversals.

Note the varied ways in which Scripture points to this

pivotal theme: "By baptism we were buried with him, and lay dead, in order that, as Christ was raised from the dead in the splendour of the Father, so also we might set our feet upon the new path of life" (Rom. 6:4); "If we died with him, we shall live with him" (2 Tim. 2:11); "Did we not feel our hearts on fire as he talked with us on the road and explained the scriptures to us?" (Luke 24:32); "Where two or three have met together in my name, I am there among them" (Matt. 18:20); "I have been crucified with Christ: the life I now live is not my life, but the life which Christ lives in me; and my present bodily life is lived by faith in the Son of God, who loved me and sacrificed himself for me" (Gal. 2:20); "Now you are Christ's body, and each of you a limb or organ of it" (1 Cor. 12:27); "Dwell in me, as I in you. No branch can bear fruit by itself, but only if it remains united with the vine" (John 15:4).

Nothing is clearer in the New Testament than that Christ is personally present in the life of the believing community and that Christianity consists essentially in participating in the cross and resurrection of Jesus. Cross and resurrection are so intrinsically linked in Scripture that it is better to think of them as a single, complex event rather than as separate events with separable meanings. The resurrection is God's yes to Christ's obedience "even unto death," and the atoning cross is the only context for grasping the significance of the Easter narratives.

At one point in his writings, Paul deliberately attempts to identify the core of the tradition he is passing on:

> Now I would remind you, brethren, in what terms I preached to you the gospel, which you received, in which you stand, by which you are saved, if you hold it fast—unless you believed in vain. For I delivered to you as of first importance what I also received, that Christ died for our sins in accordance with the scriptures, that he was buried, that he was raised on the third day in accordance with the scriptures, and that he appeared to Cephas, then to the twelve. Then he appeared to more than five hundred brethren at one time, most of whom are still alive, though some have fallen asleep. Then he appeared to James, then to all the apostles. Last of all, as to one untimely born, he appeared also to me. (1 Cor. 15:1–8 RSV)

The same theme is reworked repeatedly in the earliest documents of orthodoxy, from Ignatius and Justin Martyr to the Presbyters of Smyrna, who in A.D. 180 confessed, "We know the Son, suffering as he suffered, dying as he died, and risen on the third day, and abiding at the right hand of the Father, and coming to judge the living and the dead. And in saying this we say what has been handed down to us." The same theme echoes all the way into the language of the Westminster Confession: "All saints that are united to Jesus Christ their head, by his Spirit and by faith, have fellowship with him in his graces, sufferings, death, resurrection, and glory, and being united to one another in love, they have communion in each other's gifts and graces" (*Creeds of the Churches*, J. Leith, ed., 18, 222, 223).

Other great historical religions embody rich moral sensitivity and spiritual awareness. The Holy Spirit has worked powerfully through them. But Christianity is alone among religions in its promise of salvation from sin, guilt, and death through a relation of trust in God who becomes flesh in a living person who actually lived in history, died and was resurrected, and continues to live in the present as the animating vitality of the contemporary worshiping community. Christians everywhere of all sorts, times, languages, and cultural assumptions understand the death and resurrection of Christ as the fulcrum of their own personal faith and destiny, and the meaning of universal history. That indeed is what makes them Christians.

It is this pardoning event of cross and resurrection that is printed indelibly on the mind of the church as the crucial moment in history where we are met once for all by the redeeming God who suffers for us and delivers us from sin and death. The church's pearl of great price is its memory and present participation in the event of cross and resurrection. Those who are not grasped by this event as the decisive end-time disclosure of the meaning of human history remain, regrettably, on the outskirts of the city of faith. Those who assert that something less than God has met us in Jesus are by that Arian assertion ruling themselves out of the central stream of Christian awareness, the baptism into which we have been baptized. Those who try to conceive of Christianity without cross and resurrection do so only by ignoring what

Christians themselves have universally said about the ground of their faith and the source of their experience.

It is a sign of the overweening pride of modernity and a mark of late modern barbarism that we in the twentieth century pretend to have earned the right to judge and amend what Christians have repeatedly said constitutes the center of their consciousness. This has come only because we have supposed ourselves fully competent to creatively redesign the tradition and improve it with our supposedly superior modern imagination.

With few exceptions, the ancient ecumenical consensus held firm through the first seventeen centuries of Christianity—until modernity, when it began to fade, split, and shatter. When we limit our historical vision to modernity, there is vast confusion about where the Christian center lies. The hymns, Scripture, and liturgies of ancient Christianity continue to echo as a lovely chord through the decades of modernity, but they are perceived as anachronisms. Like the stones of Easter Island, the symbols of ancient orthodoxy remain standing amid modernity as mute witnesses to the living center once vitally known and celebrated.

It is only when we correct the myopia of modernity by the lens of a larger historical consciousness that we begin to behold the living tradition as still intact. This is done essentially as a sustained act of historical empathy.

If we bracket out modern Christianity, we find to our astonishment that we must travel far out to the periphery of the tradition into rejected esotericisms and heresies in order to find the idiosyncratic voices that today predominate and often pose as genuine Christianity. Admittedly, the views of the Gnostics, Manichaeans, Arians, Pelagians, and Socinians had local and regional influence for brief periods of time, but they never came close to meeting the criterion of Vincent of Lérins for orthodoxy, that they were everywhere, by all and always, held fast as apostolic belief.

14

Time Out: The Comic Premise of Contemporary Theology

Theology stands today in a comic relation to its subject matter (which is God, for theology remains a *logos* about *theos*). It is the most humorous of all disciplines because it has worked so hard to disavow its distinctive task. No other discipline has devoted so much energy to doing away with its own subject matter. Yet despite its hardworking earnestness, contemporary theology has never received adequate comedic analysis. It is an intricate, mostly silent, stumbling single-situation comedy, however, not witty banter.

The Cause Gap

Suppose one thinks of theology as moral advocacy. From this point of view, the dilemma of theology is the increasing scarcity of decent causes to advocate. The point is that the best causes have already been taken up and conquered by progress. The later one comes in history, the harder it is to find an original cause that has not been tampered with by past movements.

Suppose one were looking for a virgin cause. In such a situation, expansive idealism must search ever harder to find even a modestly decent cause. Eventually, with gestures of importance, it must resort to the protection of terrorist rights, the value of the graffiti movement, the right to shout profanities in one's grandmother's ear, the natural rights of sharks, and so on.

These causes offer challenges for a short time, but then the excitement seems to wane. Unfortunately, they also tend to nauseate the very religious constituencies that the exponents wish to attract, guide, guru, represent, and relegitimize. All this adds up to a "cause gap," which the ensuing discussion does its best to overcome.

Christian leadership is inevitably concerned with good causes and with the human cause, for God has taken up the cause of humanity. Meanwhile, the attesters of God's steadfast mercy amid late modern history have developed compulsive needs for ever-new causes to fuel infinitely expansive idealisms. As in an extended fuel shortage we burn up causes so fast that they are found in very short supply, yet we remain hooked on being heavy fuel users.

Another Way of Looking at Theology: The Viewpoint of Social Welfare

Thesis: *Strictly speaking, from the point of view of social welfare, there are only two types of theologians: employed and unemployed.* In previous centuries, other distinctions seemed to matter: semi-Pelagian/Augustinian, Unitarian/ Trinitarian, Arian/Athanasian, Supralapsarian/Infralapsarian. Once upon a time these distinctions made all the difference. Life and death have hung on them. Recently the more decisive distinction among theologians has not been a Christological distinction at all but an economic and sociological one? Are theologians working or not? I do not mean do they have paying jobs? I mean are they engaged in honest labor? Just think of theology rigorously from the viewpoint of the employment office and you will get what I mean.

One of my strongest motives is to put unemployed theologians back to work. The problem is made more difficult by the fact that theology appears to be one of those improbable enterprises in which, when one is not paid for doing it, one may do it even better. This is a project worth savoring, even if nothing is done about it: So I fantasize—putting unemployed theologians back to work! Splendid vision. A potentially humane service could be rendered. It might contribute to the general social welfare. It might even increase the gross national product. Or at least the dignity of labor.

The challenge heightens when one considers that it is not only the unemployed but also the employed theologians that could be put back to work again on theology. For even the employed theologians have by and large forgotten the baroque crafts and skills of theological artistry in which theologians once took such pride. Ending unemployment! What a worthwhile social vision, considered from a humanitarian point of view.

How might these vital, unemployed energies be put to work? What useful jobs are left to theologians, now that traditional (doctrinally instructive, sacramentally attentive, ecclesiastically responsive, tradition maintaining, polemically effective) theological tasks appear passé, from a modern point of view? What can theologians do with themselves as they drink the heady wines of modern freedom? In my reverie, I wonder: Might they actually have some definite calling, some urgent challenge yet to meet, or at least some little errand to run, before their final retirement from active service?

The Reluctant Advocate

I do not mean to depreciate the importance of advocacy in ministry or neglect its intricate psychological dynamics. In fact, in moments of deadliest theological boredom, we may even wonder if advocacy of a very different sort might be our emerging task—but advocacy of what?

All the best candidates for advocacy seem already to be taken up. Keep in mind that an authentic event of advocacy requires a collusion between two parties, one with a strong protective motive and another with high vulnerability and weakness. So the thought presses on us and furrows our brows: What available victim is most truly weak and vulnerable, most kicked around and despised in the modern world of religious ideas?

Suddenly we are on the track of a solution. When we put the question in that way, the answer seems surprisingly evident: the cause most despised and ignored in modern times, particularly among cultural elites, is *orthodoxy*. It seems to be the most passé, least viable, least studied, most disinteresting of all ideas. In fact, it is at the very bottom of the heap of lost causes. So, one might reason, that is where our energies as advocates might really count.

What is an attorney for? To present the client's case and protect the client's rights in the courts regardless of how he or she may feel personally toward the client. Whether the attorney is attracted to the client's smile or repulsed by the client's bad breath, limp, or surliness is irrelevant to the case. The best advocacy ignores personal feelings and states clearly the merits of the case.

Suppose we in ministry were attorneys for ancient ecumenical Christian orthodoxy in the courts of modernity. Even if there were things about these rascals (the ancient Christian exegetes, martyrs, and early church leaders) that we personally disliked, like language that seemed crude to us or habits that revolted us, still if we were conscientious attorneys solemnly charged with their defense, these personal aversions would be completely set aside. All our attention would focus on how best to present the merits of their case.

Now let us suppose that in the process of preparing their almost hopeless case for trial, we as attorneys became increasingly convinced against all our earlier predispositions that they were not only innocent, but that the proper advocacy of their case was of utmost importance to society and even to the human future. Would not we study diligently and prepare ourselves in detail for every possible contingency in argument and be able to answer all the spurious invectives that would understandably be hurled at our clients? Suppose we discovered that both judge and jury were already predisposed to view them with suspicion and unfairly discount their testimony. Would not we be dutifully bound to work all the harder to obtain the best evidence on behalf of our clients just at those times when the evidence against them seemed overwhelming?

Let us suppose that we as attorneys gradually became all the more firmly persuaded of their innocence and rightness the more deeply we delved into this strange case, even though at first we could hardly stand their garlic breath or the strangeness of the language or the oddity of their gaze. Step by step, we must establish the credibility of our witnesses, answer charges against our clients, prove that they could not have done all they are accused of, and vindicate them.

This is what makes the advocacy of these clients intriguing, stimulating, and dramatic. It is the opposite of a routine defense. Suppose we are called upon even to risk our own good reputations for such disreputable clients. Suppose something deep inside has convinced us that the case can and must be won, and its successful presentation at this juncture depends entirely upon us.

This is just the feeling that many young people in ministry are beginning to have about the case for classical Christianity. At first they took up the cause somewhat routinely and then only slowly began to be moved by it, drawn into its symbol system, claimed by its authenticity. The intense commitment of just such a conscientious attorney reveals the behavior set that we are here defining as classical Christian advocacy. It is as though these attorneys did not quite know what they were getting themselves into when they were initially assigned the case. At first they had to overcome some serious personal aversions even to serve the clients' interests. But, because they were well schooled in the ethics of advocacy, they discovered, or were discovered by, a cause that claimed their fullest energies and boldest imagination.

At last we return to the purpose of this analogy. We were merely casting about, looking only for some means of ending theological boredom and unemployment. Whether we have stumbled on it or not is for the reader to decide or reflect on. But just suppose that the most exacting empirical research turned up this reliable equation: The boredom of theology ends the moment theology takes up advocacy of the classical Christian understanding of God within the context of modern hopes and disillusionments. Vigorous, articulate advocacy is what is called for—even against heavy odds. What might be the consequences of this for biblical study, pastoral care, preaching, worship, and moral choices? The small but lively band of those who are excited and animated by this question is the subject of this discussion.

Few would quarrel with the idea that advocacy of Christian truth is the central responsibility of the pastoral office. If the idea is put that way, most would agree. But suppose we took as our subject of advocacy not modern theological opinion about Christianity but the common faith of the ancient ecumenical church gathered repeatedly in general council in its first millennium, the *consensus fidelium* that understood itself to be grounded in the heart of early Christian Scriptures. And suppose our courtroom were not merely within the confines of the church but right in the marketplaces and public arenas and enterprises of modernity itself, and even in the halls of academia?

Now we hesitate: Is the modern university a fit place for such an orthodox advocacy, or might it seem entirely out of place and embarrassing? Other types of orthodoxy most surely thrive in the university—notably Skinnerian behaviorism, Marxist orthodoxy, Freudian orthodoxy, deconstructionism, and reductive naturalism—all resting on their own fragile postulates. This leads us to muse in our quiet moments on academic freedom: Might there also conceivably be a small place still within the pluralism of the modern university for the Christian orthodoxy that spawned it?

Admittedly, the question is a little awkward and unlikely, but let us remember the essential nature of advocacy: we are not seeking to please but convince the judge, and we do not even have to admire our clients in order to defend their interests vigorously. But we may easily overestimate the tolerance of the university that so warmly claims to welcome all points of view in the marketplace of ideas. The reason ancient Christian orthodoxy is not so welcome is that it has had a history of abuse which the university, scene by scene, remembers with such explicit fixation that the larger history of nonabuse is entirely missed and subverted. This makes it all the more imperative that its defense be articulate, clear, and vigorous, if we are to obtain a fair trial.

The operating assumption of this analogy is that persons in ministry have already made a prior decision to uphold apostolic teaching. The ordained are duty bound to give this advocacy a good try. But sometimes it happens that these expected advocates put themselves in the role of bad lawyer—demanding credentials and advanced payments from their clients, rather than placing on themselves the requirement of discovering the actual merits of their case. It is apparent that sometimes a good lawyer may defend a disreputable client—but presumably those in ordained ministry have already made a fundamental decision about the good character of the client. What else could ordination imply? Yet we are still telling our clients (the apostolic witnesses) to pay us first, and then we will see if they happen to be of sufficient character to deserve our defense.

Theology as Fashion

Try another innocent fantasy. Suppose Christian teaching were considered essentially under the category of fashion. That in fact seems to be the way much "media theology" has functioned in recent times, searching breathlessly for the next new mushroom in the meadow. And we in ministry have colluded with this premise. Much of the recent energy of Christian teaching has gone into the effort first to achieve a kind of predictive sociological expertise about what is the "next new cultural wave" coming (politically, psychologically, artistically, or philosophically). Then, having spotted an "emergent movement" cresting on a distant wave, we try to imagine how we might get some small foothold for Christianity on that rolling curl so we can enjoy at least a brief ride as long as it lasts. As the torrent flows by, we then look for another emerging swell.

Does this describe recent theology? I have asked varied audiences of Christian clergy and laity that question. Each time I have been invariably reassured that the description is not unfair. It seems accurate to me, since I have fairly often experienced myself working unconsciously just in this way. Process theology and existential theology are prototypical examples, where vast theological programs have emerged to try to bend the tradition to accommodate to a Whitehead or Heidegger. At those points where the tradition does not easily accommodate, it is pronounced (note the absolute self-assurance of this act of condemnation) "irrelevant to the modern mind." The concept of hell for ideas is, according to this view, the prospect of being detached from the "intellectual momentum of our times."

Returning to the fantasy—suppose theology were fashion and we were fashion designers. Let us go all the way and imagine that we are in the company of Yves Saint Laurent, Pierre Cardin, Calvin Klein, and Dior, assembled in Paris to discuss possibilities for next year's theological market.

Suppose we, sensing this crisis of boredom, had set our heads on inventing some astonishing novelty in theology. What would be the most novel, unheard-of, and outrageous new possibility for modern theology? It is quite evident: orthodoxy. We would ask: Is it not about time for a reappearance of orthodoxy? Why? Well, because the excesses of rapid change in our industry almost require it, because people are becoming tired of everything fleeting. Cheap ideas have paraded endlessly before us, each one claiming to be an improvement on its predecessor. Each one pretends to be more now than now. It is clear, since all that has become tiresome, that the least modern option is now our best bet. That, by definition, is orthodoxy. In fact, one might say, with a wink, if theological fashion is to recover, it *must* turn to orthodoxy. Agreed.

The point of our analogy is not to show that Christian theology is like fashion or that it should begin with market research, but rather that even if it is conceived only on this least probing level of critical sensibility, at some point the designers would have to come full circle back to the classical models. But Christian teaching, of course, is least understood when it is conceived as fashion. Fashion appeals to the spirit of novelty; Christianity transmutes the very idea of novelty.

What If Orthodoxy Doesn't Fly?

I have been confidentially taken aside and gently warned by worried friends that my fascination with ancient ecumenical orthodoxy is really—well, let's face it—intolerable. Orthodoxy by any other name would smell much sweeter. They have gravely cautioned me that the whole idea is wrong, dated, and unmarketable; that it will have no effect and will be wasted effort. They have pleaded with me to say whatever curious or crazy thing I have to say but, please, in some language less embarrassing to the modern academic consensus than that of orthodoxy.

All this is amusing. Whether orthodoxy is high or low on a

Nielsen chart strikes me as a subject for a vaudeville act or a stand-up comedy. Classical Christianity has always been far less concerned with high acceptance ratings among its human audiences (including esteemed academic audiences) than with its single divine auditor. This does not imply that Christianity should masochistically wish for low ratings or hope desperately to be ignored, as it has on some occasions, but neither can it congratulate itself on the fleeting applause of the majority if that should imply a backdoor sellout of its historical memory. Rather than prudishly stomping away from this vaudeville show or abruptly switching off this comic premise, I would prefer to watch it play for a while and see whether it might be unexpectedly entertaining.

Suppose we imagine a highly imaginative young theologian, fresh out of graduate school, who has determined to begin the construction of a massive new doctrinal system solely on the basis of extensive market research into the felt needs and active hungers of the current cultural audience. (Don't laugh; it could be done.) The samples are meticulously gathered and calculated, fed into the computer, and the results are eagerly awaited. (Yes, I admit the premise is ridiculous, because it turns theology into something that it could never be—namely, public opinion analysis and salesmanship—but bear with me and see if we can learn something even from an absurd premise.) Our theologian's focus will be the accurate assessment of current cultural momentum as the sole basis of doctrinal definition. Our young genius double-checks his figures to see if they are correct. A surprising readout is beginning to print. It indicates that there apparently exists a deep itch in our society to settle things down, ask how things got this way, recover our identities, and see if we might be able to conserve and renew our more stable moral, political, and religious traditions. Further examination of these data reveals something more than a minor trend to nostalgia or sentimentality, more than the subtle influence of some incipient fascist trend in politics or the validation of some backlash theory. They appear to reveal an immense appetite for historical identity and roots in a compulsively mobile society whose magic words are *change, new, now,* and *breakthrough.*

He runs the data back through the program thinking that it

might have made a mistake, perhaps a reversal of key components of the equation. But no, on second run it is again confirmed: The actual audience for our new theological construct is amazingly different from the one we thought was there on the basis of our listening to Bultmann's description of "modern man," Tillich's concept of "correlation" with the *"kairos"*of our times, or the process theologians' estimates of prevailing *Zeitgeist*. All these standard portrayals render a profile of an audience that is extremely dissatisfied with the deadly encumbrances of tradition, insatiably thirsting for "fundamental change" based on a wholly this-worldly rejection of all supernaturalism, and so on. Our clever young market-oriented theologian then discovers to his astonishment that other eminent public opinion analysts—Gallup, Harris, Yankelovich—are coming up with similar data. The actual audience being discovered out there is one preeminently characterized by the hunger for continuity, stability, the freedom to sustain and enhance traditional values, historical identifications, and old-fashioned ways. This comes as quite a shock, because he was prepared to construct a quite different theological system based on a different expected audience profile, so it seems that a great deal of preliminary work must now be thrown out and redone.

The theological imperative of the last decade of the millennium is to reach for a higher comic vision. The current status of the academic study of religion could then be elevated to the realm of waggish slapstick or wild buffoonery or outlandish burlesque. It deserves such a place in history. This would then level the path for the recovery of the theandric premise.

15

The Winter Temperament

The Interpersonal Wilderness

With joy and sadness, we have watched the last century of the second millennium unfold decade by decade. Having made excessive promises for human self-deliverance, the twentieth century now faces the demoralization of its own unfulfilled promises.

There are many angles of vision from which to behold the failure of modern psychologies, philosophies, sciences, and politics, but the most revealing nexus of these failures, I think, lies in the impotence of modernity to sustain interpersonal covenants, to nurture responsible commitment in enduring associations and intimacies. In part, I am talking about modernity's failure to understand marriage as the most transparent clue to the failure of modern consciousness, but I could also talk about the failure of friendships and the failure of politics. Wherever I look in the interpersonal sphere I see the failure of relativized, naturalistic, narcissistic values to nurture and sustain just interpersonal relationships and responsible covenant love.

This is dramatically seen in modern marriage, especially in the popular treatment of marriage as if it were finally little more than a cost-benefit calculus, not a solemn promise in the presence of God. With that reasoning, when costs increase, the relationship ends.

Here the sexual liberationists, and many psychotherapists, despite their best intentions, have been as much a part of the problem as of its solution. The disastrous social results of modern autonomous individualism are strewn everywhere about us in the social scene. The increase in crime, social pathology, domestic violence, rape, and anomie has its roots in the loss of the primary center of social formation, the family. The diaspora of the family has its roots in the abandonment of solemnly covenanted and durably bonded matrimony. At heart, it is a theological failure, not merely a social, political, or psychological miscalculation or "setback."

I am not an alarmist about the long-term future of marriage, not only because three of four divorces end in marriage, but more so because the hunger for covenant fidelity is structured into the very nature of human sexuality. I do not wish to take an absolutely rigorous moralistic line on sexuality that admits of no exceptions. But I cannot let the subject of modernity go without attempting a pathos-laden observation that I find extremely difficult to articulate without appearing overly simplistic or judgmental. It is about divorce: The recent history of divorce is the key sign of the failure of modernity to sustain covenant accountability in the interpersonal sphere. Modernity has come to the "profound insight" that marriage is "a piece of paper," a superego intrusion, an establishment voyeurism upon two people in love. When marriage is no longer a solemnly bonded promise before God with the intent of irrevocability, it turns quickly into a moment-to-moment hedonic calculus that can be as flippantly rejected as it was entered into.

We have learned much in modernity, but we have not learned what the Old Testament calls *chesed*, the enduring, steadfast, covenant love of God that does not quit loving just because the cost-benefit ratio is lowered. Sexually, what that means for the Western moral tradition has always been and still is monogamous, enduring, covenant bonding in sexuality. We have not learned that from modern society, bent as it is toward individualistic self-assertion. We are now bedeviled by the growing awareness that we cannot sustain our family covenants on the basis of purely hedonistic values or amoral autonomy.

The interpersonal consequences of modern self-assertive

narcissism are not just minor disorders or regrettable errors, but on the whole they are more accurately described as calamitous. The reason this has not been sooner recognized and squarely confronted by religious leaders is precisely because their accommodationist predilections have severely reduced critical perception. For modernity still persists in fantasizing history as a progressive evolution toward ever-better forms wherein our most vexing moral ills will finally be cured through improved education, technology, and moral suasion. This talk continues precisely while society is falling to pieces.

One who begins with these ideological blinders will fail to see the social disasters that follow in the wake. For one has already decided that such disasters cannot really persist in a truly modern world with all its obvious intellectual, moral, and educational resources.

The Winter Temperament

The premise of this book is that it is possible for the core of classical Christian belief to stand in critical dialogue with modern personal and social hopes, but this cannot be a mere monologue, as it has recently been, in which Christians listen to modernity without making any distinctive positive contributions. It is in an effort to overcome the one-sidedness of this conversation that I place special emphasis now upon the recovery of the apostolic center. That does not imply an abandonment of the task of dialogue, but rather hopes in a deeper way for real dialogue.

I have spent much of my professional life as a teacher working span by span on a bridge between psychology and religion. Just how incessantly preoccupied I have been with this theological bridge is clear, if from nothing else, from the titles of my previous books: *Kerygma and Counseling, Contemporary Theology and Psychotherapy, The Structure of Awareness, The Intensive Group Experience, After Therapy What?, Game Free, TAG: The Transactional Awareness Game,* and *Guilt-Free.* After two decades of bridge building, however, it is finally dawning on me that the traffic is moving on the bridge only one way: from psychological speculations to rapt religious attentiveness.

The conversation has been completely one-sided. Theology's listening to psychology has been far more accurate, empathic, and attentive than has psychology's listening to theology. I do not cease to hope for a viable two-way dialogue, but there is as little evidence that theology is ready to speak out in such a dialogue as there is that psychology is ready to listen. The bridge will not be built by the complete acquiescence of Christianity to the reductionist assumptions of psychology, or by relinquishing such key religious postulates as providence and resurrection.

We have been going, as Jeremiah said, "backwards and not forwards" (Jer. 7:24). We eat but are not satisfied (Lev. 26:26). We are technologically superior to premodernity, but not psychologically, morally, spiritually, and certainly not interpersonally. "He that soweth iniquity shall reap vanity" (Prov. 22:8 KJV).

Having "sown the wind," we are now "reaping the whirlwind" of interpersonal alienation and discontent. We have looked to the modern academic and clinical centers to tell the church what it is supposed to be doing, and what its values are, only to find that "if one blind man guides another they will both fall into the ditch" (Matt. 15:14). At the height of our supposed powers, we as moderns "stumble at noon day as in the night; we are in desolate places as dead men" (Isa. 59:10 KJV). Like Jeremiah, we behold the once-fruitful land that, contrary to all our expectations, has become an interpersonal wilderness.

Sometimes it seems that only a few may survive the desolations of modernity. Yet it was recalled in the New Testament that "God waited patiently in the days of Noah and the building of the ark, and in the ark a few persons" were "brought to safety through the water" (1 Peter 3:20). Even as the remnant that survived the destruction of Rome were the sons and daughters of the Christian martyrs of the second and third centuries, so the remnant that survives modernity may have to go through (God help us) trial by fire.

It is the winter season for rigorous Christian teaching. But it has been through many winters before. It is time to cast off all things unessential, to drop leaves and branches that are no longer functional, to trim down for a long winter of survival, to reduce energies to the bare essentials in order to sustain the organism through the hazards of time.

There is much stormy weather ahead. Only the hardiest may survive. Modernity is a winter season for classical Christianity. Spring will come, but only to those who have survived the winter.

We have heard a great deal in our time about a theology of conviviality, the feast of fools, the laughter of God, the celebration of the body, and so forth—but we know better. Most modern religious talk about these themes has been under the sway of hedonistic philosophies that deal with suffering only by avoidance.

There is indeed a joy in the Christian life that comes from discipline, a laughter that echoes even under winter's heaviest snows, a happiness that Christians know to be grounded in God's own joy over creation. But it is never easily won or sustained without effort. Young Christians especially seem to sense that the season of late modernity is a winter season and that it is time for conserving the essentials.

Epilogue: The Collage

The ink remained bold and clear on an ancient papyrus manuscript. It had survived many centuries with thoughtful care, though repeatedly handled and read aloud countless times by persons awed by its beauty and sacredness. But years ago the old manuscript was set on a shelf, and then inadvertently pushed to the back, into a corner where it sat out decades of neglect. In that drafty spot the delicate manuscript was subjected to harsh extremes of heat and cold. Dust accumulated. Mice nibbled at its edges. In time a steady unnoticed drip eventually made the ink wash and fade.

Thinking it was nothing, a janitor tossed the manuscript into the throwaway cart, which was then set outdoors for pickup just before a heavy rain, which caused the characters to wash away even more. One could hardly make them out.

Meanwhile, a contemporary artist, rummaging through the bin looking for interesting materials for his newest collage, ran across this fascinating role of fragile papyrus. He viewed it aesthetically as a lovely piece of antique parchment. He was especially attracted by its fine texture, its off-white color, the swirling flows of ghost-gray markings. Excitedly he carried the bundle home, spread it out, and decided instantly that it could serve as just the right backdrop material for a large collage that would significantly display twisted fragments of industrial junk and waste on the background of a lovely ancient-looking surface.

Suppose that you and I became the proud owners of this collage and hung it in the most honored place, only later to discover, on closer inspection, that the sporadic markings of ink were actually complex hieroglyphs that proved to be an ancient sacred scripture that held the promise of revealing significant insight into human history and destiny. What would then be our task? First to try to remove painstakingly the heavy modern overlay without damaging the fragile script and then to restore the faded letters so as to make them visible and understandable again.

Many may still persist in viewing Christianity essentially as an object of aesthetic interest, a curious yet lovely modern collage, without reference to its historical identity, its power to redeem, or its radical claim on the human spirit. The happy task of theology is to rediscover and reveal the message underneath the garish modern overlay.

Appendix:
Perennial Resources for Ministry

This appendix addresses the practical problem of building a personal, pastoral, or church library that will make available to the community of faith key texts of classical Christianity. Several obstacles stand in the way. Many important works are unavailable at any cost. Some are available only in expensive editions. Even the ones that are available on order are seldom found on the shelves of bookstores. Stores that have some minimal stock in classical Christian writings often limit it to a particular denominational tradition or doctrinal perspective. So we must learn to order books.

Among classic Christian authors whose key works are either completely inaccessible, available only on rare-book lists, or in completely inadequate translations or editions are: Albert the Great, Alexander of Hales, Robert Bellarmine, Theodore Beza, Carlos Borromeo, Guillaume Farel, August Hermann Francke, Johann Gerhard, Jean Gerson, Hugh of St. Victor, John Knox, Hugh Latimer, William Laud, Peter Lombard, Raymond Lull, Luis de Molina, Theodore of Mopsuestia, and Nikolaus von Zinzendorf, to mention a few. The list could continue much further. Ten years after the original publication of this book, these resources remain largely unavailable.

The happier side of this picture is that even though many classical texts are out of print, some are nonetheless available, and many at an exceptionally low cost. The purpose of this bibliography is to help persons of limited means to build a personal or church library of key classical texts without inordinate expense. The criteria I have applied in recommending the following are: listing only primary sources in reliable editions; listing only books in print, to save the reader's search time; keeping costs down by preferring inexpensive or paperback editions to high-cost reprints; limiting the list to widely acknowledged classics; attempting to express the full variety to central Christian traditions without partisan prejudices.

The result is encouraging. It is possible to build a "no frills" classical Christian library with a modest investment. The key, of course, is selective ordering, and an astute book retailer can be of immense help in placing these special orders. The list is organized chronologically, ending with anthologies and multivolume series.

Primary Sources of Classical Christianity

The Apostolic Fathers

Early Christian Writings. Translated by M. Staniforth. New York: Penguin Books, 1968.

The Faith of the Early Fathers. Translated by W. A. Jurgens. Collegeville, Minn: Liturgical Press, 1970.

Apostolic Fathers, Justin Martyr and Ireneus. Ante-Nicene Fathers, edited by A. C. Coxe, vol. 1. Grand Rapids, Mich.: Eerdmans Publishing Co., 1956.

The Apostolic Fathers. Edited by Jack N. Sparks. Nashville: Thomas Nelson, 1978.

Hermas, Tatian, Athenagoras, Theophilus,. Clement of Alexandria. Ante-Nicene Fathers, vol. 2.

Ante-Nicene Fathers

Alexandrian Christianity. Edited by H. Chadwick. Library of Christian Classics, vol. 2. Philadelphia: Westminster Press, 1954.

Origen. *On First Principles*. Translated by G. W. Butterworth. Gloucester, Mass.: Peter Smith, 1966.

Tertullian, Parts I–III. Ante-Nicene Fathers, vol. 3.

Hippolytus, Cyprian, Caius, Novation, Appendix. Ante-Nicene Fathers, vol. 5.

Early Latin Theology. Edited by S. L. Greenslade, Library of Christian Classics, vol. 5, 1956.

Early Christian Fathers. Edited by H. Bettenson. Oxford: Oxford University Press.

Major Patristic Writings

The Seven Ecumenical Councils. Edited by H. R. Percival. Nicene and Post-Nicene Fathers, 2d series, vol. 14.

Athanasius, St. *Select Works and Letters.* Edited by A. Robertson. Nicene and Post-Nicene Fathers, 2d series, vol. 4. Grand Rapids, Mich.: Eerdmans Publishing Co., 1956.

Athanasius, St. *The Resurrection Letters.* Edited by Jack N. Sparks. Nashville: Thomas Nelson, 1979.

Basil, St. *Letters and Select Works.* Edited by B. Jackson. Nicene and Post-Nicene Fathers, 2d series, vol. 8.

Cyril of Jerusalem, St. *Catechetical Lectures.* Edited by E. H. Gifford; and Gregory Nazianzen, St. *Orations and Letters.* Edited by C. G. Browne and J. E. Swallow. Nicene and Post-Nicene Fathers, 2d series, vol. 7.

Gregory of Nyssa. *Dogmatic Treatises.* Edited by V. W. Moore and H. A. Willson. Nicene and Post-Nicene Fathers, 2d series, vol. 5.

Gregory of Nyssa. *From Glory to Glory.* Edited by H. Musurillo. Crestwood, N.Y.: St. Vladimir's Seminary Press, 1979.

Eusebius. *The History of the Church.* Translated by G. A. Williamson. Grand Rapids: Baker Books, 1975.

Chrysostom, St. John. *In Praise of St. Paul.* Boston: Daughters of St. Paul, 1964.

Chrysostom, St. John. *On the Priesthood; Ascetic Treatises; Select Homilies and Letter; Homilies on the Statues.* Nicene and Post-Nicene Fathers, 2d series, vol. 9.

Augustine, St. *Confessions of St. Augustine.* Translated by E. B. Pusey. New York: Macmillan, 1961.

Augustine, St. *Enchiridion on Faith, Hope, and Love.* Edited by H. Paolucci. Chicago: Henry Regnery Co., 1961.

Augustine, St. *St. Augustine: On Education.* Edited by G. Howie. Chicago: Henry Regnery Company, 1969.

Augustine, St. *City of God.* Translated by J. Healey. New York: E. P. Dutton and Co., 1956.

Augustine, St. *On Christian Doctrine*. Translated by D. W. Robertson. Indianapolis: Bobbs-Merrill Co., 1958.

Augustine, St. *First Catechetical Instruction*. Translated by J. P. Christopher. New York: Paulist Press, 1946.

Augustine, St. *Augustine: Early Writings*. Edited by J. H. Burleigh. Library of Christian Classics, vol. 6. Philadelphia: Westminster Press, 1953.

Augustine, St. *The Writings Against the Manichaeans and Against the Donatists*. by A. H. Newman, R. Stothert, and C. D. Hartranft. Nicene and Post-Nicene Fathers, 2d series, vol. 4.

Jerome, St. *Letters and Select Works*. Edited by W. H. Fremantle. Nicene and Post-Nicene Fathers, 2d series, vol. 6.

Hilary of Poitiers, St. *Selected Works*. Translated by E. W. Watson; and John of Damascus, St. *Exposition of the Orthodox Faith*. Translated by S. D. F. Salmond. Nicene and Post-Nicene Fathers, 2d series, vol. 9.

Ambrose, St. *Selected Works and Letters*. Edited by H. de Romestin. Nicene and Post-Nicene Fathers, 2d series, vol. 10.

Severus, Sulpitius, *Works*. Edited by Alexander Roberts; Vincent of Lerins. *Commonitory*. Edited by C. A. Jeurtley; Cassian, John. *Works*. Edited by E. C. S. Gibson. Nicene and Post-Nicene Fathers, 2d series, vol. 11.

Leo the Great, Gregory the Great. Edited by C. L. Feltoe. Nicen and Post-Nicene Fathers, 2d series, vol. 12.

Boethius, *The Consolation of Philosophy*. Translated by V. E. Watts. New York: Penguin Books, 1976.

Benedict, St. *Rule*. Translated by J. McCann. Westminster, Md.: Christian Classics, Inc., 1972.

Dionysius the Areopagite. *Divine Names and Mystical Theology*. Translated by C. E. Rolt. Naperville, Ill.: Alec R. Allenson, 1920.

Maximus the Confessor. *The Church, the Liturgy and the Soul of Man*. Still River, Mass., St. Bede's Publications, 1982.

John Climacus, *The Ladder of Divine Ascent*. Boston: Holy Transfiguration Monastery, 1978.

The Philokalia. Edited by Elizabeth A. Clark. Wilmington: Michael Glazier, 1983.

Sayings of the Desert Fathers. Translated by B. Ward. Kalamazoo, Mich.: Cistercian Publications, 1975.

Women in the Early Church. Edited by Elizabeth A. Clark. Wilmington: Michael Glazier, 1983.

Women and Religion: A Feminist Sourcebook of Christian Thought. Edited by Elizabeth Clark and Herbert Richardson. New York: Harper & Row, 1977.

Western Asceticism. Edited by Owen Chadwick. LCC, vol. 12.

Later Christian Fathers. Edited by H. Bettenson. Oxford: Oxford University Press.

Classical Medieval Texts

Anselm, St. *Basic Writing.* Translated by S. N. Dean. La Salle, Ill.: Open Court Publishing Co., 1966.

Fairweather, E., ed. *A Scholastic Miscellany: Anselm to Ockham.* Library of Christian Classics, vol. 10, 1956.

Hildegaard of Bingen. *Symphonia.* Edited by Barbara Newman. Ithaca: Cornell University Press, 1988.

Bernard of Clairvaux. *Treatise on Loving God.* Kalamazoo, Mich.: Cistercian Publications, 1974.

Francis of Assisi, St. *Writings.* Chicago: Fransciscan Herald Press, 1964.

Francis and Clare: The Complete Works. CWS. Paulist Press. 1982.

Bonaventura, St. *The Soul's Journey Into God, The Tree of Life, and the Life of St. Francis,* CWS, Paulist Press.

Thomas Aquinas, St. *Nature and Grace, Selections from Summa Theologica.* Edited by A. M. Fairweather. Library of Christian Classics, vol. 11, 1954.

Thomas Aquinas, St. *Political Ideas of St. Thomas Aquinas.* Edited by D. Bigongiari. New York: Macmillan Publishing Co., 1973.

Thomas Aquinas, St. *Summa Contra Gentiles.* Translated by A. Pegis, J. F. Anderson, V. J. Bourke, and C. J. O'Neil. Notre Dame, Ind.: University of Notre Dame Press, 1975.

Thomas Aquinas, St. *Summa Theologiae,* vol. 1; *The Existence of God,* Part 1, Questions 1–13. Edited by Tho. Gilby. New York: Doubleday & Co., 1969.

Eckhart, Meister. *Complete Works.* CWS. New York: Paulist Press.

Julian of Norwich. *Showings.* CWS. New York: Paulist Press.

Thomas à Kempis, *The Imitation of Christ.* Edited by F. W. Farrar. New York: E. P. Dutton & Co., 1976.

Catherine of Genoa. *Purgation and Purgatory, The Spiritual Dialogue.* CWS. New York: Paulist Press.

Reformation and Counter-Reformation Classics

Luther, Martin. *Selected Writings of Martin Luther.* 4 vols. Edited by Theodore G. Tappert. Philadelphia: Fortress, 1967.

Luther, Martin. *Selections From His Writings.* Edited by John Dillenberger. New York: Doubleday & Co., 1961.

Luther and Erasmus: Free Will and Salvation. Edited by E. G. Rupp and P. S. Watson. LCC, 1969.

What Luther Says. Edited by E. Plass. 3 vols. St. Louis, MO: Concordia, 1959.

Works of Martin Luther: An Anthology. 6 vols. Philadelphia: Muhlenberg Press, 1943.

Zwingli & Bullinger. Edited by G. W. Bromiley. LCC.

Simons, Menno. *Complete Writings.* Edited by J. C. Wenger. Scottsdale, Pa.: Herald Press, 1956.

Melanchthon & Bucer. Edited by W. Pauck. LCC.

The Book of Concord (1580). Edited by T. G. Tappert. Philadelphia: Fortress Press, 1959.

Calvin, John. *Institutes of the Christian Religion.* Edited by J. T. McNeill. Library of Christian Classics, vol. 20–21, 1960.

Council of Trent, 1545–63, Canons and Decrees. Translated by H. J. Schroeder. St. Louis: B. Herder Book Co., 1955.

Teresa of Avila, St. *The Way of Perfection.* Edited by E. A. Peers. New York: Doubleday & Co., 1973.

Ignatius de Loyola, St. *Spiritual Exercises.* Translated by A. Mottola. New York: Doubleday & Co., 1964.

Post-Reformation Classics

More, P.E., and Cross, F.L., eds. *Anglicanism.* London: SPCK, 1962.

Hooker, Richard. *Of the Laws of Ecclesiastical Polity.* New York: E. P. Dutton & Co., 1954

Wollebius, J.; Voetius, G.; Turretin, F. *Reformed Dogmatics.* Edited by J. W. Beardslee. Grand Rapids, Mich: Baker Book House, 1977.

Spener, Philipp J. *Pia Desideria.* Translated by T. G. Tappert. Philadelphia: Fortress Press, 1974.

Bunyan, John. *Pilgrim's Progress.* New York: Penguin Books, 1965.

Henry, Matthew. *A Commentary on the Whole Bible.* 6 vols. Iowa Falls, Iowa: World Bible Publishers, n.d.

Pascal, Blaise. *Pensees.* Translated by W. F. Trotter. New York: E. P. Dutton & Co., 1958.

Law, William. *A Serious Call to a Devout and Holy Life, The Spirit of Love.* CWS. Paulist Press.

Wesley, John. *Works of the Rev. John Wesley.* Edited by Thomas Jackson. 14 vols. London: Wesleyan Conference Office, 1872.

Wesley, John. *The Works of John Wesley.* Edited by Frank Baker. Bicentennial Edition. 9 vols. to date. Nashville, TN: Abingdon, 1975–. (Formerly published by Oxford Unviersity Press.)

John Wesley's Theology: A Collection from His Works. Edited by Robert W. Burtner and Robert E. Chiles. Nashville: Abindgon: 1982.

Edwards, Jonathan. *The Works of Jonathan Edwards.* 2 vols. Carlisle, Pa: Banner of Truth Trust, 1984.

Schleiermacher, Friedrich. *Brief Outline of the Study of Theology.* Translated by T. N. Tice. Atlanta, Ga.: John Knox Press, 1966.

Schleiermacher, Friedrich. *The Christian Faith.* Edited by H. R. Mackintosh and J. S. Stewart. New York: Harper & Row, 1963.

Schleiermacher, Friedrich. *On Religion: Speeches to Its Cultured Despisers.* Translated by John Oman. New York: Frederick Ungar Publishing Co., 1955.

Doctrinal Theology of the Evangelical Lutheran Church. Edited by Heinrich Schmid. 3d ed. Minneapolis, MN: Augsburg, 1899.

Reformed Dogmatics. Heinrich Heppe. Translated by G. T. Thomson. London: George Allen and Unwin, 1950.

John Henry Cardinal Newman. *Works*. Edited by Joseph Rickaby. Westminster, MD: Christian Classics Inc., 1977.

General Anthologies of Shorter Selections

Bettenson, H., ed. *Documents of the Christian Church*. Oxford: Oxford University Press, 1970.

Denzinger, H., ed. *Sources of Christian Dogma (Enchridion Symbolorum)*. Translated by Roy Deferrari. New York: Herder, 1954.

Forell, George, ed. *Christian Social Teachings*. Minneapolis: Augsburg Publishing House, 1971.

Kehoe, Kimball, ed. *Theology of God: Sources*. New York: Bruce Publishing Co., 1971.

Leith, John L., ed. *Creeds of the Churches*. Atlanta, Ga.: John Knox Press, 1979.

Neuner, N., and Dupuis, J., ed. *The Christian Faith: In the Doctrinal Documents of the Catholic Church*. New York: Alba House, 1981.

Stephenson, J. ed. *Creeds, Councils, and Controversies: Documents Illustrative of the History of the Chruch A.D. 337–461*. Nashville: Abingdon, 1988.

Multi-Volume Critical Editions of Classical Christian Text

Baillie, J., McNeill, J.T., and Van Dusen, H.P., eds. *Library of Christian Classics* (LCC). 26 vols.

Deferrari, R.J., ed. *The Fathers of the Church*. 73 vols. to date. Washington, DC: Catholic University Press, 1947–.

Dillenberger, John, ed. *A Library of Protestant Thought*, 13 vols. New York: Oxford University Press, 1964–1972.

Elder, E. R., editor. *Cistercian Fathers Series*. 44 vols. to date. Kalamazoo, MI: Cistercian Publications, 1968–.

Page, T.E., et al., eds. *The Loeb Classical Library*. Cambridge, Mass.: Harvard University Press.

Payne, Richard J., ed. *Classics of Western Spirituality*. 30 vols. to date. Mahwah, NJ: Paulist Press, 1978–.

Quasten, J., and Plump, J. C., and Burghardt, W., ed. *Ancient Christian Writers*, The Works of the Fathers in Translation. 44 vols. New York: Paulist Press, 1946--.

Roberts, A., and Donaldson, J., eds. *Ante-Nicene Fathers*, 10 vols.

Schaff, P., ed. *Creeds of Christendom*. 3 vols. Grand Rapids: Baker, 1985.

Schaff, Philip, ed. *Nicene and Post-Nicene Fathers of the Christian Church*. First Series, 14 vols.; Schaff, Philip and Henry Wace, eds. Second series, 14 vols.

Abbreviations

AEG	Ante-Nicene Exegesis of the Gospels. 6 vols. Edited by Harold D. Smith. London: S.P.C.K., 1925.
AFT	Agenda for Theology. Thomas C. Oden. San Francisco: Harper & Row, 1979.
ANF	Ante-Nicene Fathers. Edited by A. Roberts and J. Donaldson. 10 vols. 1885–1996. Reprinted ed., Grand Rapids: Eerdmans, 1979. Book (in Roman numerals) and chapter or section number (usually in Arablic numerals), followed by volume and page number.
BC	The Beginnings of Christology: A Study of Its Problems. Willi Marxsen. Philadelphia: Fortress, 1969.
BHT	The Bible in Human Transformation. Walter Wink. Philadelphia: Fortress, 1973.
BSG	The Birth of the Synoptic Gospels. Jean Carmignac, transl. Michael J. Wrenn. Chicago: Franciscan Herald Press, 1987.
CD	Church Dogmatics. Karl Barth. Edited by G. W. Bromiley, T. F. Torrance, et al. 4 vols. Edinburgh: T. & T. Clark, 1936–1969.
CG	City of God. Augustine. NPNF 1 II.
CH	Church History. Eusebius of Caesarea. NPNF 2 I. See also EH.
Comm.	Commentaries. John Calvin. 22 vols. Edinburgh: Calvin Translation Society, 1921. Reprinted 1981.
CWS	Classics of Western Spiritually. 30 vols. Edited by R. Payne. Mahwah, N.J.: Paulist Press, 1978—.
Doc.Vat.	The Documents of Vatican II. Edited by W. M. Abbott. New York: America Press, 1966.

DT   Dogmatic Theology. Francis Hall. New York: Longmans, Green, and Co., 1907–1922.

EC   Evangelical Christology. Bernard Ramm. Nashville: Thomas Nelson, 1985. Or Henry Clay Sheldon. The Essentials of Christianity. New York: George H. Doran, 1922.

EHCM   The End of the Historical-Critical Method. Gerhard Maier. St. Louis: Concordia.

FNTC   The Foundation of New Testament Christology. Reginald H. Fuller. New York: Scribners, 1965.

H&B   The Historian and the Believer. Van A. Harvey. New York: Macmillan, 1966.

HCTIS   Historical Criticism and the Theological Interpretation of Scripture. Peter Stuhlmacher. St. Louis: Concordia.

JGM   Jesus—God and Man. Wolfhart Pannenberg. Philadelphia: Westminster, 1968.

JMF   Jesus Means Freedom. Ernst Käsemann. Philadelphia: Fortress, 1969.

JR   Journal of Religion

KJKEK   *Das Kreuz Jesu und die Krise der Evangelischen Kirche.* Edited by S. Findeisen, H. Frey, W. Johanning. Bad Liebenzwell: Verlag der Liebenzeller Mission, 1967.

KuD   Kerygma und Dogma

LCC   Library of Christian Classics. Edited by J. Baillie, J. T. McNiell, and H. P. van Dusen. 26 vols. Philadelphia: Westminster, 1953–1961.

NPNF   A Select Library of the Nicene and Post-Nicene Fathers of the Christian Church. 1st Series, 14 vols. 2nd series, 14 vols. Edited by H. Wace and P. Schaff. References by title and book or chapter, and susection, and NPNF series no., volume and page number. New York: Christian, 1887–1900.

NQHJ   A New Quest for the Historical Jeus. James M. Robinson. Naperville: Allenson, 1959.

NTGW   The New Testament: A Guide to Its Writings. Günther Bornkamm. Ann Arbor: University of Michigan Press (microfilm), n.d.

PG   The Proof of the Gospel. Eusebius. Edited by W. J. Ferrar. Grand Rapids: Baker, 1981.

PS	Parochial and Plain Sermons. 8 vols. Works of John Henry Cardinal Newman. Edited by Joseph Rickaby. Westminster, MD: Christian Classics Inc., 1977.
PW	Practical Works. Richard Baxter. 23 vols. London: James Duncan, 1830, or
PW	The Power of the Word. John Breck. St. Vladimir's Seminary Press, 1987.
RGG	Religion in Gegenwart und Geschichte
RO	Radical Obedience: The Ethics of Rudolf Bultmann. Thomas C. Oden. Philadelphia: Westminster, 1966.
TC	Training in Christianity. Søren Kierkegaard. Princeton: Princeton University Press, 1941.
TNT	Theology of the New Testament, 2 vols. Rudolph Bultmann. New York: Scribner's, 1952. A Theology of the New Testament. George E. Ladd. Grand Rapids: Eerdmans, 1974.
W	Weimarer Ausgabe, Dr. Martin Luthers Werke. Kritische Gemsamtausgabe. Weimar: Hermann Boehlau, 1883– .
WLS	What Luther Says. Edited by E. Plass. 3 vols. St. Louis, MO: Concordia, 1959.

Index